THE COMING OF
THE SON OF MAN

When Jesus Returns to Gather

His Bride to Heaven

Jeffrey R. Horton

ISBN 978-1-63575-389-9 (Paperback)
ISBN 978-1-63575-390-5 (Digital)

Christian Faith Publishing, Inc.
296 Chestnut Street
Meadville, PA 16335
www.christianfaithpublishing.com

All scripture references are taken from the New King James Version unless otherwise stated.

Printed in the United States of America

For as the lightning comes from the east and flashes to the west, so also will the coming of the Son of Man be.

—Matthew 24:27

Contents

SECTION 1

The Witness from Mount Olivet

1

Let's Get Caught Up

This is the third book in the *Emmaus Road* series. The first two books are entitled *See the Day Approaching* and *Daniel's Seventieth Week*. Unless you have read the first book in this series, it is quite possible that you will not understand the phrase *see the Day approaching*. You might think that it means the kind of *day* that can be singled out on the calendar. So let's get caught up.

God's Prophetic Week

The New Testament apostles understood such Day-terms in the context of God's Week of prophetic thousand-year Days. Since so much of end-time prophecy is spoken from the perspective of this great Week, we need to take a moment and bring everyone up to speed.

The first-century apostles realized that God counts a thousand years of our time as being *a prophetic Day in His sight*. This revelation was not meant to dismiss the importance of time but to *mark time* instead. In this way, He has given us the key to understanding the prophetic *times and seasons* as they relate to the Lord's first and second coming.

The sacred chronology of the Old Testament Scriptures reveal that there were four thousand years, or *four prophetic Days*, from the creation of Adam *to the start of Jesus's ministry at age thirty.*

This means that His anointed ministry coincided with the dawning of the fifth great Day and set the *last three Days* of God's great Week in motion. In the Bible, these final three Days are called *the last Days.*

They were not meant to be understood as the last days of the Old Testament era nor as a recent development in end-time prophecy. Instead, they are thousand-year Days. As such, the Church has always lived in the last Days.

Therefore, in Luke 13:32–33, Jesus said that He would build His church, add to His body, and court His bride for *two prophetic Days* (or two thousand years). On the third Day, His Church, Body, and Bride would be complete.

Together, these six prophetic Days (four for the Old Testament and two for the Church age) bring us to the *seventh great Day*, when Jesus will return to catch up His Church, Body, and Bride to reign with Him for a thousand years. Jesus called this *the last Day* in John 6:39, 40, 44, and 54. This last Day is also called *the Day of the Lord* in Scripture.

These Day-terms are important, for as I have already noted, much of end-time prophecy is spoken from the perspective of this great Week. Therefore, the phrase "as we see the Day approaching" in Hebrews 10:25 refers to this final thousand-year Day, not a lone day on the calendar.

"That Day" includes a thousand years' worth of events, beginning with His second coming in the rapture, then His treading at the battle of Armageddon three and one-half years later, and finally, the destruction of death itself at the end of the thousand years. This is the amount of time predetermined by God to restore heaven's kingdom over the earth *by putting every enemy underfoot.*

This mission will begin when Jesus returns. Since He promised that "those who overcome" will reign with Him as kings and priests during the thousand years, the first order of business will be to catch His Bride up to heaven.

Once we are all there, we will be officially installed as the heavenly government seated with Christ at the Father's right hand. This authoritative grant will set the last three and one-half years of Daniel's seventieth week in motion.

Daniel's Seventieth Week

Those who read the second book in this series can understand why it would be unscriptural to call this a midtribulation rapture in such a scenario. This is because a time of future tribulation lasting a mere seven years *cannot be found in Scripture*. This becomes clear once we realize that the prophecy in Daniel 9:24–27 *is all about Christ's first and second coming.* It is not a prophecy about the Antichrist at all, even though the coming of this "man of sin" is firmly established in other prophecies.

The true interpretation of Daniel's prophecy reveals that the first half of the seventieth week was fulfilled by Jesus's anointed ministry in which He taught, healed the sick, and performed miracles for three and one-half years.

In the middle of the week, He brought a Sabbath end to the need for sacrificial offerings under the Law. He accomplished this by offering Himself once and for all as God's sacrificial Lamb on the cross. God ratified this everlasting covenant by raising Jesus from the dead.

At that point, the prophecy was temporarily suspended or "put on hold." This was due to the fact that the Jewish nation rejected Jesus as their Messiah Prince. Thus, the rest of the prophecy could not be fulfilled at that time, not until they confess, "Blessed is He who comes in the name of the Lord."

During this prophetic pause, Jesus has been building His Church, growing His Body, and courting His Bride. The second half of the week will resume when Jesus returns after two Days to seize His Church, Body, and Bride up to heaven. This event will spark

Israel's third-Day revival predicted in Hosea 6:1–2, *"After two Days He will revive us, on the third Day He will raise us up."*

As the Lord's "heavenly Esther," we will intercede together with "our Husband King" to ensure that the Antichrist's wicked plot to destroy Israel is foiled. This will use up the first three and one-half years of our thousand-year reign. We will continue to judge the earth in that *appointed Day*[1] until every enemy has been thoroughly put underfoot.

The Restoration of End-Time Terms

The scriptural view of Daniel's seventieth week also restores the prophetic value of certain terms. These terms were corrupted by subtracting Christ from Daniel's prophecy in lieu of the Antichrist. We found that the term *abomination of desolation* actually refers to the fall of Jerusalem shortly after the time of Christ. This resulted in the destruction of the Jewish Temple in AD 70.

This prophetic event triggered a time of great and unparalleled tribulation *that has continued to this very hour.* Like the apostle John, we have always been companions in *the tribulation.*[2] Therefore, "the tribulation" does not refer to a future period lasting a mere seven years. Instead, it is a lengthy period spanning the better part of the last two millennia.

Our second book also pointed out that the Scriptures link the coming of the Antichrist with a different event altogether, an event called *the transgression of desolation.* We learned all about this event by comparing the vision of "the little horn" in Daniel 8 with Paul's comments about the coming "man of lawlessness" in 2 Thessalonians 2.

Even though the terms *abomination of desolation* and *transgression of desolation* are very similar, the Scriptures present a sharp contrast between these two events. Our failure to understand the

---

[1]   Acts 17:31

[2]   Revelation 1:9

difference has resulted in a lot of unnecessary confusion concerning the end times.

Nowhere is this more evident than how people have interpreted Jesus's end-time teaching in His Olivet Discourse. Without a doubt, this teaching is one of the most misunderstood texts in the whole of the Bible.

For one thing, the fact that Jesus referenced *the abomination of desolation* and *great tribulation* in His teaching led many to assume *that it was all about the final years of the Antichrist.* We projected a false seven-year tribulation upon His teaching and thought that the great tribulation was a future event to be fulfilled during those final years.

For many, this meant that Jesus was no longer speaking to His Church but to the Jews left behind after the rapture. Thinking that we were reading about the Antichrist's final years, we then concluded that this present age must end with the battle of Armageddon and the second coming of Christ.

So in order to maintain the truth that believers will be "caught away" *prior* to the battle of Armageddon, we invented a secret and signless coming in the rapture that could supposedly happen at any moment. This was unnecessary, for Jesus's Olivet Discourse reveals that the rapture *is the second coming of Christ* and that it will occur several years before the battle of Armageddon.

Would it surprise you to learn that the battle of Armageddon appears nowhere in Jesus's Olivet Discourse? Nor is there any mention of the Antichrist, the mark of the beast, his image, or any other event associated with the last half of Daniel's seventieth week. Why is that? Could it be that Jesus was teaching about the rapture instead? Is there a better way to understand the Olivet Discourse?

2

Who Needs a DVD?

The following incident occurred as Jesus and His disciples left the Temple during His final week in Jerusalem. At the time, His disciples did not realize that Jesus would be crucified *in just two more days*.

> As Jesus was leaving the Temple, one of His disciples said to Him, "Look, Teacher! What massive stones! What magnificent buildings!"
>
> "Do you see all these great buildings?" replied Jesus. "Not one stone here will be left on another; every stone will be thrown down."
>
> As Jesus was sitting on the Mount of Olives opposite the Temple, Peter, James, John, and Andrew came to Him privately. "Tell us," they said, "when will this happen, and what will be the sign of your coming and of the end of the age?"[1]

---

[1] Composite of Mark 13:1–3 and Matthew 24:3 (NIV)

The end-time lesson that followed is called *the Olivet Discourse*. We call it that simply because Jesus gave this teaching while He sat on the Mount of Olives with four of His closest disciples. The significance of this teaching is enormous. It is a record of what Jesus Himself taught about His own return. Who wouldn't want to sit with the Master in a private session to hear Him teach about end-time prophecy?

If Only We Had a DVD

Imagine how awesome it would have been if the world had today's technology in Jesus's time. One of the four disciples could have used his cell phone to make a video recording of what Jesus taught that day. If such a recording had been preserved and passed down to succeeding generations, we could all just watch a DVD of the Olivet Discourse and hear it all firsthand.

But as wonderful as that would have been, we have something just as valuable, *if not even better*; for we have, not one, but three separate accounts of the same teaching—one from Matthew, another from Mark, and a third from Luke.[2]

Since each word in all three accounts was inspired and selected by the Holy Spirit Himself, we have in effect three "records" of the same message—*all from God Himself*.

This advantage becomes even more pronounced when we consider that the Holy Spirit did not merely duplicate the account word for word three times. Instead, He restated it three times *using a variety of words and terms* that have similar meanings.

So unlike having a DVD recording wherein the message is only stated once, we can turn to one of the other two accounts and get another slant on what was actually said. If there is a word or phrase that we don't quite understand in one account, we can bet that one of the others will clarify it for us. When all three accounts are read

---

[2]   Matthew 24, Mark 13, and Luke 21

and compared together, we should have no trouble understanding what Jesus taught.

Three Parallel Accounts

With that said, it is important to understand that all three accounts follow *the same outline of what Jesus actually taught.* Each describes *the same scenario of events* and *in precisely the same order or sequence.*

So from a practical standpoint, we can take any segment of Jesus's teaching, cross reference it with the other two, and thereby understand any term or part that might be questionable.

Once we are able to grasp what Jesus taught, the sequence of events spanning the entire time of the Church until Christ's return at the end of this age becomes crystal clear.

Luke's Advantage

While all three synoptic Gospels were written and widely circulated prior to the destruction of the Jewish Temple in AD 70, it is generally accepted that Luke's *was the last to appear on the scene.* This is significant, for Luke accompanied the apostle Paul on several of his mission trips.

Since these two spent a lot of time together on the mission field, what do you think they talked about when they were not actively ministering?

Most certainly, Paul took advantage of their time together to pour what he knew into the heart of Luke. No doubt this included everything that Paul knew about the Lord's return. Because of this, Luke was privy to the insights and revelations that Paul had received from the Lord about end-time prophecy, *including what Jesus taught when He sat with His disciples on the Mount of Olives.*

This probably explains why the Holy Spirit enlisted Luke to write a third account. The Spirit of God wanted us to get Paul's insights on what Jesus meant when He taught that day.

Since Paul was specifically called to preach to the Gentiles, Luke's account proves to be extremely helpful for a non-Jewish audience that might not be as familiar with certain terms used by the Old Testament prophets.

This is especially critical when it comes to the term *the abomination of desolation*. Because of Luke's account, we know that Paul linked this term with the forthcoming destruction of the Jewish Temple, not with the coming of the Antichrist as so many teach today.

This is important, because the misidentification of this term discolors our entire understanding of what Jesus actually taught from the Mount of Olives. We will think that Jesus was teaching about the final few years of the Antichrist when He was not. We will miss what Jesus said about the rapture and confuse His second coming with the events associated with the battle of Armageddon several years later.

We will not realize that Jesus actually used this impromptu meeting as an opportunity to unveil something that no one had ever heard of before, an event so unusual and so spectacular that it almost defies our imagination. Today, we call it the rapture, but back then they called it *the gathering*.

As we will see, Jesus's teaching was actually intended to reveal how He will come to gather His Bride to heaven at the end of this age. It reveals how His "elect" (the Church) will miss the snare of that Day to "escape" and "stand in His Presence."

It's Time to Get It Right

Without a doubt, Jesus's Olivet teaching is one of the most misunderstood teachings in the Bible. This is because we have not availed ourselves of the true value of Luke's account.

The result has been a lot of unnecessary confusion in the Church as it concerns the rapture and the second coming of Christ. It contributed to the idea of a posttribulation rapture in which the Church will remain to suffer and endure the final years of the Antichrist.

On the other hand, those who embrace other views of the rapture must overlook the scriptural connection between "our being gathered" and the coming Day of the Lord. This is unfortunate, because the relationship between these two events *proves why we will miss* the mark of the beast, the worship of his image, and the wrath of God that will be poured out upon the nations.

When rightly interpreted, Jesus's Olivet Discourse retains the key advantages purported to be gained by either a pretribulation or midtribulation rapture. In fact, these benefits are more solidly upheld and further strengthened.

The advantage is that now we have a view that stands the test of the whole of Scripture. We do not need to ignore certain passages that complicate our position or twist the meaning of a given word or verse until it fits with our overall scheme. Instead, we can maintain contextual integrity, stay true to the meaning of the Greek words, and let Scripture interpret Scripture.

It is time to get it right. It is time to take advantage of Paul's keen insights concerning these things as portrayed in Luke's worthy account. With Christ's return so near, we can no longer afford so many differing and mutually exclusive views. *There is a better way.* And the world needs to hear a clear and certain message in this critical hour. As the apostle Peter said,

> And so we have the prophetic word confirmed,
> which you do well to heed as a light that shines
> in a dark place, until the Day dawns and the
> Morning Star rises in your hearts… for prophecy never came by the will of man, but holy men
> of God spoke as they were moved by the Holy
> Spirit.[3]

---

[3]   2 Peter 1:19–21

We can, therefore, consider these three Gospel accounts just as valuable as having a live recording of Jesus's Olivet teaching. And while a DVD would have been awesome, we can still get the original message, *plus an inspired commentary or two, all for the price of one!*

3

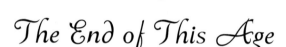

The End of This Age

The bewildered disciples approached Jesus on the Mount of Olives and asked two important questions: *"When will these things happen?"* and *"What will be the sign when all these things will be fulfilled?"* In order to understand what "things" they were referring to, we must consider the context of events that led up to this meeting in the first place.

Jesus and His disciples had just left the Temple for the final time prior to His arrest and crucifixion. Having been ultimately rejected by the Jewish nation at large, Jesus responded by uttering two fateful pronouncements that day.

The first was that their "House" (or Temple) was left to them desolate and that not one stone would be left standing upon another. The second was that the nation of Israel would not see Him again until they confessed, "Blessed is He who comes in the name of the Lord."

So in essence, the disciples wanted to know when the Temple would be destroyed and when Israel would see Jesus again. Immediately, the fact that we have three inspired accounts works to our advantage, for the questions are a bit vague in the accounts of Mark and Luke. Matthew, however, was inspired to write the second question as, *"What will be the sign of your coming and of the end of the age?"*

The manner in which the Holy Spirit moved Matthew to word this question is extremely significant. It tells us that this age will end with the second coming of Christ. In fact, the same sign that signals His coming also signals the end of this age.

This truth might sound like a no-brainer until we realize that *the Scriptures also link the end of this age with the rapture.* Our first book presented the overwhelming evidence from the Scriptures that Jesus will return in the rapture as the sixth great Day from Adam ends and the seventh Day dawns. This seventh Day is *the last Day* of God's prophetic Week for mankind.

This is the phrase that Jesus used when He referred to the resurrection of believers, saying, "Everyone who sees the Son and believes in Him has everlasting life, *and I will raise him up at the last Day.*"

Jesus was not talking about the last twenty-four-hour day the world will ever know but the last prophetic thousand-year Day. Such terms are meant to be understood from God's perspective of prophetic time. They were meant to be understood in the context of God's great Week.

This last Day is called the Day of the Lord. It marks the time of Christ's millennial reign. Since Jesus promised that overcoming believers *will reign with Him for the thousand years,* the rapture must happen at this time. We will not reign with Him *until we have been glorified with Him.* This explains why Jesus associated this last Day with the resurrection of those who have believed on Him.

We can say then that His coming, the rapture, and the end of this age are all linked *to the end of the sixth prophetic Day.* Simply put, this present age will end with the dawning of the seventh great Day from Adam, when the Day of the Lord begins.

Bear in mind that the Scriptures also place the rapture *several years before the battle of Armageddon* as well. This explains why the Holy Spirit reworded Matthew's question. He wants us to understand that this age will end with the second coming of Christ in the rapture.

In other words, He wants us to realize that it is wrong to link the rapture, the second coming of Christ, and the end of this age *with the battle of Armageddon.* The issue is not whether Jesus will descend with the armies of heaven to destroy the Antichrist. Indeed, He will. The issue is whether this represents "another coming." And as we will see, it does not.

Later in His teaching, Jesus said, "But he who endures *to the end* shall be saved. And this gospel of the kingdom will be preached throughout the world as a witness to all nations, *and then the end will come.*"

It should be obvious that "the end" means *the end of this age.* This means that the Church will remain to preach the Gospel throughout the world until the end of this age (or the sixth great Day). So when Jesus said, "He who endures to the end shall be saved," He was not talking about those who must endure and outlast the Antichrist *after the rapture.* Instead, he was referring to believers whose bodies will be redeemed *at the rapture*—when He comes in that Day. The apostle Paul wrote,

> When He comes in that Day to be glorified in His saints and to be admired among all those who believe... [1]

Why the End Is Not Armageddon

Those who read the second book in this series should be able to understand why the rapture *must predate the battle of Armageddon by three and a half years.* At the rapture, Jesus will stand on the Mount of Olives and split it in two. According to Zechariah 14:5 and Revelation 12:6–14, the remnant of Israel will flee through this mountain valley and be kept from the Antichrist *for this same period of time.*

Obviously, the Antichrist is still active on the earth, for his ultimate destruction at the battle of Armageddon will not happen until

---

[1]   2 Thessalonians 1:10

the end of these three and a half years. *This means that the battle of Armageddon is an event properly assigned to the seventh Day and the age to come.*

This agrees with Scripture, for Christ's millennial reign is for the purpose of "putting every enemy underfoot." Or we could say it like this: *He comes* so that His Bride can reign with Him. He *reigns* until every enemy is made His footstool.

And then there is the passage in Isaiah 66:7–8. Verse 7 clearly depicts the birth of a male Child "before the nation of Israel was in labor" and "before her pain came." This *pain-free* birth represents the resurrection of Christ. In contrast, the companion passage in Revelation 12:1–5 depicts the birth of a male Child as the woman "cries out in labor and in pain to give birth."

Once "born," this Child is immediately caught up to God's throne in heaven. This *painful* birth represents the rapture. The "catching up" of the male Child uses the same Greek word that Paul used to describe the rapture in his second letter to the Thessalonians. The word is *harpazo* in both instances.

Back in Isaiah's prophecy, the next verse (verse 8) refers to the rapture by saying, "the earth shall be made to give birth in one day" and "a nation will be born at once." At the rapture, Jesus will force the dust of the earth to give up its claim on the bodies of those who have died in Christ.

We who are alive and remain shall also be changed and caught up to officially meet the Lord in the air. In other words, a nation of kings and priests will be *born* or "birthed from death" all at once. *Combined, these two births yield "one new Man."*

Flipping back to Revelation 12, the passage reveals that the Church will be caught up to God's throne just as Israel begins their flight from the Antichrist and is kept for three and a half years. This three and a half years is the last half of Daniel's seventieth week.

Why Armageddon Is Not the Second Coming

So several years before the battle of Armageddon takes place, the following events will have already occurred: the Lord will have come, the rapture will have already been accomplished, and this present age will have come to an end.

Since the rapture is connected to the end of this age, it will not be a sign-less event. *The same sign that signals the end of this age also signals the Lord's coming—and therefore the rapture as well.*

In essence, we have confused Christ's second coming, an end-of-the-age event, with His mission of putting every enemy underfoot, a seventh-Day event. To say it as simply as possible, we have confused "His coming" with "His reigning."

The apostle Paul gave us God's perspective of the difference between "coming" and "reigning" when he was inspired to write about resurrection: "But each one in his own order (or turn): Christ the firstfuits, afterward those who are Christ's at His coming."

The phrase "those who are Christ's at His coming" refers to the rapture of His Church, Body, and Bride. The next three verses describe what will happen once Jesus has come a second time to take His Bride to heaven to rule with Him in that seventh Day.

> Then comes the end [of the thousand years], when He delivers the kingdom to God the Father; when He puts an end to all rule and all authority and power; for He must reign till He has put all enemies under His feet. The last enemy that will be destroyed is death. (1 Cor. 15: 24–26, NIV; emphasis added)

To exclude the Antichrist from the phrases "all rule," "all authority and power," and "all enemies" is a great mistake. Therefore, when we say that Christ's millennial reign *will not begin until the Antichrist is destroyed at Armageddon*, we alter what the passage actually says. In effect, we change "He must reign *until*" to mean "He will reign *after*."

We must remember that the age to come relates to the last thousand-year Day. In Acts 17:31, it is "the appointed Day" in which "the Man whom God has ordained" will judge or rule the world in righteousness.

In the Old Testament, the judges of Israel delivered Israel from her enemies and ruled before the nation had kings. Judges 3:9–10 says that "the Lord raised up a deliverer (Othniel) for the children of Israel." Then he "went out to war, and the Lord delivered the king of Mesopotamia into his hand."

Likewise, Jesus will come and "raise us up" to reign with Him. Together, we will "go out to make war" against the Antichrist. Don't confuse His coming *at the seventh Day* with His treading *during the seventh Day.*

The Age to Come

Since Jesus's coming in the rapture marks the end of this age, we were also meant to understand that *the seventh Day is also called the age to come.*

The truth that this *last Day* is "the age to come" can be seen by comparing a couple of passages of Scripture. First, the passage in Hebrews 6:4–5 reveals that those who have become enlightened, who have tasted the heavenly gift, who have become partakers of the Holy Spirit, and have tasted the good word of God, have also been *tasting the powers of the age to come.*

These "powers" did not pass away with the early Church. We are still sampling these spiritual powers in our day and time via the gifts of the Spirit. Not only that, they will be *fully operative in the age to come.* Think about it, if the past two thousand years have just been a foretaste, what glorious power can we expect to be manifested in the age to come?

There is, however, another passage to consider, for Paul also referred to a time when these powers would *cease and no longer be required*—when "that which is perfect has come."[2]

> But whether there are prophecies, they will fail; whether there are tongues, they will cease; whether there is knowledge, it will vanish away; for we know in part, and we prophesy in part. But when that which is perfect has come, then that which is in part will be done away.

This "perfect and eternal state" refers to eternity future in a new heavens and a new earth. It will begin once death has been abolished at the end of Christ's thousand-year reign. Once death itself has been vanquished *and there are no more yokes to break*, the anointing to break such yokes will no longer be required.

Now follow the logic. Since we are presently living near the end of the sixth great Day, the only future period that stands between us and the elimination of death *is the seventh Day*. There is no other prophetic age or period of time that can both "come" and then "pass away" other than the seventh Day.

Therefore, the lapse of the sixth Day will end this present age. The seventh Day marks the age to come. The bottom line is that this present age will end *with the second coming of Christ and the rapture of the Church, not the battle of Armageddon.*

---

[2]   1 Corinthians 13:8–10

4

The Beginning of Birthing Pains

Jesus began His Olivet teaching by giving the disciples a preliminary overview of what believers should expect to see during this present age until He returns. Since all three Gospel accounts are so similar for this part of His teaching, we'll use Matthew's account for now.

> Take heed that no one deceives you. For many will come in My name, saying, "I am the Christ" and will deceive many. And you will hear of wars and rumors of wars. See that you are not troubled; for all these things must come to pass, but the end is not yet.
>
> *For nation will rise against nation, and kingdom against kingdom. And there will be famines, pestilences, and earthquakes in various places. All these are the beginning of sorrows.*[1]

---

[1] Matthew 24:4–8

Jesus referred to these things as the beginning of "sorrows." In Greek, the word is *odin*, which literally means "birth pains." Jesus revealed that this two-Day pause in the middle of Daniel's seventieth week would be characterized as a time of sorrows, birthing pains, and travail.

We know that these birth pains are not reserved for a future seven-year period of tribulation because Paul acknowledged their existence back in his time.

> For I consider that the sufferings of this present time are not worthy to be compared with the glory which shall be revealed in us. For the earnest expectation of the creation eagerly waits for the revealing of the sons of God... for we know that the whole of creation groans and labors with birth pangs until now.
>
> Not only that, but we also who have the first fruits of the Spirit, even we ourselves groan within ourselves, eagerly waiting for the adoption—the redemption of our body.[2]

Paul wisely understood that the world would continue to suffer the tribulations and trials that Jesus described as birth pains *while the earth awaits the birth or manifestation of the sons of God.* The word *birth* in this sense refers to the kind of resurrection that produces a glorified immortal body—*one that can never taste death again.*

Next, Jesus revealed that His followers would also experience great persecution until He returns. Mark's Gospel states,

> But watch out for yourselves, for then they will deliver you up to councils, and you will be beaten in the synagogues. You will be brought before rulers and kings for My name's sake, for a testimony

---

[2]   Romans 8:18–23

to them. And the gospel must first be preached
to all nations.

But when they arrest you and deliver you up,
do not worry beforehand, or premeditate what
you will speak. But whatever is given you in that
hour, speak that; for it is not you who speak, but
the Holy Spirit.

Now brother will betray brother to death, and a
father his child; and children will rise up against
parents and cause them to be put to death. And
you will be hated by all for My name's sake. But
he who endures to the end shall be saved.[3]

The other two Gospel accounts contain similar statements.
Matthew adds the ominous prediction that "because lawlessness will
abound, the love of many will grow cold."

In his second letter to Timothy, the apostle Paul expanded on
this part of Jesus's teaching by saying, "But know that in the last
Days perilous times will come: for men will be lovers of themselves,
lovers of money, boasters, proud, blasphemers, disobedient to parents, unthankful, unholy, unloving, unforgiving, slanderers, without
self-control, brutal, despisers of good, traitors, headstrong, haughty,
lovers of pleasure rather than lovers of God."[4] Obviously, Paul did
not worry about being "politically correct."

Jesus also likened this time to the days of Noah. One of the
outstanding features of Noah's time was that the earth was "filled
with violence." This characteristic is repeated twice, once in Genesis
6:11 and again in 6:13. Can anyone dispute the accuracy of these
predictions today?

"You" and "They"

---

[3]   Mark 13:9–13
[4]   2 Timothy 3:1–4

It is important to understand that throughout Jesus's Olivet teaching, "you" refers to believers looking for His return while "they" refers to either the unbelieving Jews, the unbelieving Gentiles, or to both.

I think we can all agree that watchful believers, both then and now, are the ones who would be "beaten in synagogues," "brought before rulers," who would "speak by the Spirit," and who would be "hated by all nations for the name of Jesus," not the unbelieving Jews and Gentiles of either their time or ours.

This principle remains constant throughout His teaching, even when Jesus said, "Therefore when *you* see the abomination of desolation… then let those who are in Judea flee to the mountains… " *Since this was a first-century event*, Jewish Christians were still living in Jerusalem at that time.

Therefore, it was proper to say, "Pray that *your* flight may not be in winter or on the Sabbath." Unlike so many today, they still respected God's law of the Sabbath even though they were no longer under the law.

The unbelieving Jews, on the other hand, proudly thought that God would not allow their city to be destroyed. They rejected Jesus's admonition to flee and were trapped within the city during the entire length of the siege.

Luke, therefore, added, "And *they* will fall by the edge of the sword and be led away captive into all nations." The pronoun obviously refers to the nation of Israel. *They* were the ones that fell by the edge of the sword, not the Church.

Jesus's statement that believers would see the abomination of desolation does not mean that the Church will remain on the earth during the final years of the Antichrist as some teach. It does not mean that you will have to confront the "image of the beast," fear the "mark of the beast," or stock up on "tribulation food" in order to survive until "the end."

Such teachings are merely the result of well-meaning believers who have not understood the terms that Jesus used in His teaching. We don't have to manipulate the pronouns as if Jesus was talking to Jewish believers who missed the rapture. We don't have to invent a secret coming or take His teaching out of context in order to preserve a rapture-position in which we escape the snare of that Day.

When that Day dawns, this present age will end, and we will be caught up to heaven. We will not be here to experience these seventh-Day events when the age to come begins.

Jesus went on to say, "And there will be signs in the sun, in the moon, and in the stars… then *they* will see the Son of Man coming in a cloud with power and great glory. Now when these things begin to happen, look up and lift up *your* heads, because *your* redemption draws near.[5]

We don't need a secret coming, for His visible coming will result in *our* redemption, not *theirs*. *They* will see Him and mourn. In contrast, *we* will see Him and rejoice!

Only those of us who have the first fruits of the Spirit will receive the redemption of our bodies that the whole of creation has been groaning to see birthed. After all, isn't this what birthing pains are all about—the birth or manifestation of the sons of God?

In summary, Jesus provided an overview of what we as believers should expect to see during our two-Day preaching assignment. He said that we would see birth pains, suffer persecution, and experience tribulation until the end of this age. Nevertheless, by His grace we would thrive and successfully preach the gospel of the kingdom throughout the world.

As we will see, Jesus never made any direct references to the Antichrist in His Olivet teaching. Nor did He mention any of the events that will happen during the final few years of the beast. He said nothing about the battle of Armageddon either. People only assumed that He did when they saw the term abomination of desolation.

Since the thousand-year "Day of His coming" will begin with the rapture, any event after that, including those associated with the final years of the Antichrist, *is properly assigned to the age to come.*

---

[5]   Luke 21:27–28

5

Not One Stone Left Standing

Jesus began His teaching by giving His disciples a general overview of this present age. He spoke of *the beginning of sorrows* or *birth pains*. These sorrows would result from false religious figures, wars and rumors of wars, famines, pestilences, and earthquakes in various places—*things that have been with us since the first century of the Church.*

He assured His disciples that even though they would be persecuted from day one until the end, this would not prevent those who believed on Him from preaching the Gospel throughout the world.

Next, Jesus proceeded to answer their specific questions. The first question concerned the impending destruction of the Temple. "When will this happen?" "And what sign will signal that it is about to happen?"

Jesus explained that their answers could be found in the prophecies of Daniel concerning "the abomination of desolation."

The prophecies in the book of Daniel not only explained *why* the Temple would be destroyed *but provided the time frame for its destruction as well.* In essence, the prophecies revealed that it would be destroyed due to Israel's rejection of their Messiah Prince. As far the time frame, it would be destroyed before "that fateful generation" would pass away.

It is, therefore, no coincidence that the next section in each of the three Gospel narratives begins by describing *the abomination of desolation* and the tribulation to follow. The Gospel of Mark continues by saying,

> So when you see the abomination of desolation, spoken of by Daniel the prophet, standing where it ought not (let the reader understand), Then let those who are in Judea flee to the mountains. Let him who is on the housetop not go down into the house, nor enter to take anything out of his house. And let him who is in the field not go back to get his clothes.
>
> But woe to those who are pregnant and to those who are nursing babies in those days! And pray that your flight may not be in winter.
>
> For in those days there will be tribulation, such as has not been since the beginning of the creation which God created until this time, nor ever shall be.

Matthew's account is virtually identical except that he adds the adjective "great" to describe the time of unparalleled tribulation to follow. Both accounts highlight the event called "the abomination of desolation," noting that the reader should understand.

Those who were familiar with the Old Testament prophets would have known that this prophetic term appears in Daniel 9:26–27, Daniel 11:31–35, and Daniel 12:10–12. They also would have known that this event was a common theme in many other prophecies, including Deuteronomy 28:47–68, Leviticus 26:27–46, and Ezekiel 5:5–17 to name just a few.

In essence, the prophets revealed that God would judge Israel on account of their abominations by bringing an army against

Jerusalem, by destroying their Temple fortress, and by driving them into captivity among the nations for a lengthy period of time.

Jesus was well aware of these prophecies, emphasizing them quite often during His final week in Jerusalem. In fact, just before He arrived, Jesus viewed the city from afar and wept for the city saying,

> If you had known, even you, especially in this your day, the things that make for your peace! But now they are hidden from your eyes.
>
> For the days will come upon you when your enemies will build an embankment around you, surround you and close you in on every side, and level you, and your children within you, to the ground; and they will not leave in you one stone upon another, because you did not know the time of your visitation.[1]

Jesus knew that the words of the prophets concerning the fate of Israel would shortly come to pass. He was weeping for *their generation*, knowing that these things would happen *in their lifetime*.

Since these prophecies were so abundant throughout the Old Testament Scriptures, the mere mention of the term abomination of desolation only required a parenthetical footnote to "let the reader understand."

Unfortunately, this is not true today. Our "Gentile slant" on Daniel's prophecy of the seventy weeks corrupted the true meaning of this term. We subtracted Christ from the prophecy and added the Antichrist in His place.

Because of this, prophecy teachers now link a first-century event that is already past with the coming of the Antichrist, as though the abomination of desolation still remains in our future. We built much of our end-time scenario based on this faulty premise.

---

[1]   Luke 19:43–44

Fortunately, the Holy Spirit gave us a third Gospel account in order to avoid such confusion. I surmise that He knew future generations would misinterpret this part of Jesus's Olivet lesson, "rock the boat" so to speak, until we are all "tossed about by every wind of doctrine."

Luke Calms the Storm

Up to this point in the Olivet Discourse, Luke has merely restated the same thoughts expressed by Matthew and Mark. But from this point on, his account provides several important contributions, particularly with respect to the abomination of desolation and the gathering of Christ's elect in the rapture.

Luke was a Gentile by birth, well educated in Greek culture, and a physician by profession. Most importantly, he was a dear friend of the apostle Paul (Col. 4:14), his fellow worker (Philemon 24), and fellow missionary. He was with Paul from his second missionary trip until his first imprisonment in Rome. Luke was the loyal friend who remained with Paul after all the others had deserted him (2 Tim. 4:11).

The fact that Luke spent a considerable amount of time under the tutelage of Paul is an important point worth noting. This is especially so when we consider the fact that the Holy Spirit thought it necessary to add a third account of the Olivet Discourse—*one commissioned to be written by Paul's protégé.*

There can be no doubt that Paul passed on the end-time revelations he had received by "the word of the Lord" to Luke during the time they spent together. This becomes evident when the rest of Luke's account is compared to those of Matthew and Mark.

Since Luke obviously shared Paul's commitment to preach the Gospel to the Gentiles, we should not be surprised that Luke thought it necessary to clarify the term *abomination of desolation.* A Jewish reader well versed in the prophecies of Daniel might be content with "let the reader understand," but not a Gentile.

Therefore, rather than merely duplicate what was said in the other two accounts, Luke clarified this part of the discourse by quoting Jesus as saying, *"But when you see Jerusalem surrounded by armies, know that its desolation is near."* By cross-referencing the three accounts, we can understand that the abomination of desolation was fulfilled when the Roman armies laid siege to Jerusalem from AD 66–70.

By restating this segment of Jesus's teaching, the Holy Spirit confirmed what we learned about the abomination of desolation from Daniel's seventieth week—the truth that this event was associated with the generation of Jesus's time, not with a future Antichrist near the approach of the seventh Day.

We know that the abomination of desolation was a first-century event, because Luke's account links these things with the scattering of Israel to the nations.

> Then let those who are in Judea flee to the mountains, let those who are in the midst of her depart, and let not those who are in the country enter her. For these are the days of vengeance, that all things which are written may be fulfilled. But woe to those who are pregnant and to those who are nursing babies in those days!
>
> For there will be great distress in the land and wrath upon this people. And they will fall by the edge of the sword, and be led away captive into all nations. And Jerusalem will be trampled by Gentiles until the times of the Gentiles are fulfilled.

Luke's account uses the same verbiage as Matthew and Mark as far as warning those in Judea to flee. He quotes the same woe to pregnant and nursing mothers as do the other accounts.

Those who have read the second book in this series understand why Jesus emphasized "this woe" in connection with the abomination of desolation. The siege of Jerusalem lasted for three years and part of a fourth. With their food supply completely cut off, the people trapped inside the city eventually resorted to cannibalism in an attempt to survive.

It has nothing to do with a future Antichrist. Instead, it describes the horrors of a generation that were so desperate that they ate their own children to stay alive. No wonder Jesus wept.

6

The Wise Shall Understand

The advantage of having three Spirit-inspired accounts of the Olivet Discourse means that we can now define the term *abomination of desolation* with absolute certainty. We only needed to cross-reference this segment of Jesus's teaching with whichever account made it any clearer.

When we did, we found that Luke's account defined it as the time when the Roman armies would take their stand against Jerusalem and lay siege to the city. This three-and-one-half-year siege resulted in the destruction of the Jewish Temple, with not one stone left standing. And with that, Jesus answered the first question posed by His disciples.

Today, people confuse the issue. Matthew and Mark quoted Jesus as saying that the abomination of desolation would be seen "standing in the holy place" and "standing where it ought not."

The Greek word for *standing* is *histemi*. It is the same word used in Matthew 2:9, when the star of Bethlehem came from the East and went before the wise men until it "stood" over where the young child was. The star was a sign. *Likewise, the arrival of the Roman armies was a sign that Jerusalem's desolation was near.*

Today, our western minds read about an abomination standing in the holy place and conclude that Jesus was talking about the "image of the beast" being set up in a rebuilt Jewish Temple.

Jesus was not referring to an image being set up by a future Antichrist but to an embankment being built around the holy city by the Romans. This army, along with its imposing embankment, would be seen "standing in the holy place and where it ought not."

Let the Reader Understand

In His teaching, Jesus advised His disciples to do a study in the book of Daniel concerning the abomination of desolation. Their time together was running out, and with the cross still before them, there was only so much that they could perceive in the time that was left.

So He pointed them to the prophecies that would answer their questions more fully. He knew that when they did, they would *see themselves in those very prophecies.* He knew that His Spirit would give them understanding so that they could be strong and "do great exploits."

Did you know that the Church of the book of Acts can be found in the same prophecy that describes the abomination of desolation? Shall we do what the founding apostles did and "study it out"?

The prophecy in Daniel 11:31–35 begins by saying,

> And forces shall be mustered by him, and they shall defile the sanctuary fortress; they shall take away the daily sacrifices and place there the abomination of desolation.

The prophecy revealed how forces (the Roman armies) would be mustered against the "sanctuary fortress." This is a fitting description of the Temple in Jesus's time, for it was located within a fortress so impenetrable that it took the Roman armies more than three years to prevail against it.

Daniel's prophecy further revealed that "they would defile the sanctuary fortress, take away the daily sacrifices, and place there the abomination of desolation." Who was the prophet talking about? Was he referring to the Roman Legions, the Jews of Jesus's time, or a future Antichrist in our time?

It becomes clear when we study the Hebrew words that the Holy Spirit chose to use. "To place" is *nawthan*, meaning "to bring forth" or "cause." Was it not Israel's "abominations" and rebellion that ultimately brought forth the Roman armies and caused the desolation?

"Take away" is the Hebrew word *soor-soor*. It means to "turn aside from" or "let fail." *Young's Literal Translation* of this part of the prophecy states, "And have polluted the sanctuary, the stronghold, and have turned aside the continual [sacrifice], and appointed the desolating abomination."

Who polluted the sanctuary and made it a den of thieves? Did the Roman Legions do that? Did they turn away from the daily offerings and let them fail? What does history record?

As an eyewitness to the siege, the Jewish historian Josephus recorded the exact date that the temple sacrifice failed, noting that "on the seventeenth day of Panemus the daily sacrifice had failed, and had not been offered to God for want of men to offer it; and that the people were grievously troubled at it" (Wars, VI. 2.1).

These things happened in AD 70. Between the severity of the famine and the violence of the rival Jewish factions fighting among themselves, no priests were able to perform the daily offerings. *And so the offerings simply failed.*

These events fulfilled the prophecy in Daniel 12:11–12 concerning the length of the siege and the 1,290 days until the failure of the daily sacrifice. The extra forty-five days marked the end of the siege, when Titus finally gained possession of the last stronghold and granted clemency to the remaining survivors.

Therefore, Daniel's prophecy points to the Jewish priests and occupants trapped inside the sanctuary fortress during the siege of Jerusalem, not a future time involving the Antichrist.

The prophecy links to Jesus's pronouncement that their Temple had become desolate, no longer "His Father's House," for they had made it a den of thieves.

This desolation has continued now for nearly 1,900 years. To date, the Temple Mount in Jerusalem still stands void of a Temple. It remains desolate to this day.

Long ago, a Greek translation of the Old Testament was made called the *Septuagint*. Interestingly, it translates the passage in Daniel 9:27 by saying, *"And upon the temple shall be the abomination of desolation; and at the end of the time (age) an end shall be put to the desolation."*

Be Strong and Do

The prophecy in Daniel 11 continues in verse 32 by giving us a glimpse of Spirit-empowered believers as they emerged from the upper room on the Day of Pentecost.

> Those who do wickedly against the covenant he shall corrupt with flattery, but the people who know their God shall be strong and carry out great exploits.
>
> And those of the people who understand shall instruct many, yet for many days they [the people of Israel] shall fall by the sword and flame, by captivity and plundering.

The prophecy revealed that even though the nation of Israel would "fall by the edge of the sword and be led away captive into the nations," there would be a remnant from among their own people that would "know their God."

Jesus told His disciples, "I am the way, the truth, and the life. No one comes to the Father except through Me. If you had known

Me, you would have known My Father also; and from now on you know Him and have seen Him."[1]

Ultimately, His disciples finally *understood.* From then on, they began to "instruct many" by preaching the Gospel, first in Jerusalem, then in Judea and Samaria, and eventually to the ends of the earth.

Daniel's prophecy said, "But the people who know their God shall be strong and carry out great exploits." The Hebrew text literally reads, "But the people who know their God shall be strong and do."

The translators added "great exploits" thinking that the sentence needed a clearer ending. But men like Luke and Paul understood it just fine. Luke would eventually record these great exploits in the sequel to his Gospel account. The book became known as "the book of *Acts.*" Luke considered it to be simply a continuation of "all that Jesus *began both to do and teach.*"

Daniel's prophecy concerning the abomination of desolation concludes in verse 35 by saying,

> And some of those of understanding [Christians] shall fall [be martyred] to refine them, purify them, and make them white, until the time of the end, because it is still for the appointed time.

We now know that "the appointed time of the end" refers to the end of this present age. It is an appointed time, marked by the seventh prophetic Day—*the Day that we can see approaching.*

The phrase "make them white" relates to the martyrs portrayed in the fifth seal of the book of Revelation.

> When He opened the fifth seal, I saw under the altar the souls of those who had been slain for the word of God... then a white robe was given to each of them... [2]

---

[1] John 14:6–7

[2] Revelation 6:9–11

7

"Before" and "After"

As we can see, properly identifying the abomination of desolation is critical to Jesus's Olivet Discourse. It determines whether Jesus was talking about the coming of the Son of Man or the coming of the son of perdition.

The fact that Daniel's prophecies associate this term with first-century events effectively eliminates any direct mention of the Antichrist from Jesus' discourse.

Even though Jesus spoke of a plurality of "false Christs" and "false prophets," He made no direct mention of the Antichrist himself. Why did Jesus fail to mention him if His teaching was supposedly about the Antichrist's final years?

In fact, when the entire discourse is read, we find that Jesus said nothing about the mark of the beast, the image of the beast, the false prophet, or the two witnesses anywhere in His teaching.

Other events are noticeably absent as well, such as the fall of Babylon, the seven trumpets and bowls of God's wrath, and perhaps most significantly, the battle of Armageddon itself.

And yet so much of our end-time doctrine is built around the misunderstanding that the Olivet Discourse is all about the final years of the Antichrist.

It should now be obvious that the abomination of desolation does not refer to a future event connected with the Antichrist, but to a past event that befell the Jewish people of Jesus's time.

Jesus did not ignore the question posed by His disciples. He was faithful to tell them how their Temple would be destroyed. If not here, then in what segment of His response did He ever answer their question?

All three Gospel accounts also confirm the truth that this singular event inaugurated a unique time of great and unparalleled tribulation never to be repeated again. This time of unequaled tribulation started back then *and has been going on ever since.*

Since then, the world has endured false prophets, false religions, world wars, cold wars, atomic bombs, the threat of nuclear annihilation, racial violence, ethnic cleansings, mass genocide, the use of chemical weapons on innocent women and children, Nazi concentration camps, worldwide terrorist attacks, severe earthquakes, flooding tsunamis, third-world famines, devastating pestilences, and the unrelenting persecution of Christians throughout the world. And the list could go on and on.

There are those among us who would confuse the issue by saying that the great tribulation is coming. Some even teach that the Church will have to outlast the Antichrist. *I'm here to tell you that in fact, the tribulation is nearly over.* As we will see, it is about to be cut short for the sake of Christ's elect as the dawn of the seventh Day approaches.

Immediately after, but Just before

The truth that the time of great tribulation is about to end can be seen by comparing two important prophecies. The first one comes from the prophet Joel. In Acts 2:20, Peter quoted this critical prophecy on the Day of Pentecost.

> The sun shall be turned into darkness, and the
> moon into blood, before the coming of the great
> and awesome Day of the Lord.

The second one comes from Jesus's Olivet teaching. In Matthew 24:29, He prophesied,

> Immediately after the tribulation of those days the sun will be darkened, and the moon will not give its light; the stars will fall from heaven, and the powers of the heavens will be shaken.

Jesus prophesied that the signs of celestial darkness in the sun, moon, and stars would occur *immediately after* the tribulation of those days. In the context of His teaching, the "tribulation of those days" refers to what we now know to be a lengthy time of great and unparalleled tribulation. It began with the abomination of desolation back in the first century and continues to this day.

Joel, on the other hand, predicted that this same sign of celestial darkness would occur *before the coming of the Day of the Lord.*

When we combine these two "before" and "after" statements, we get the full revelation: *Immediately after the tribulation of those days, but before the Day of the Lord, the sun, moon, and stars will be darkened.* In other words, these celestial signs will herald *the end* of the great tribulation and *the advent* of the Day of the Lord. Since the Day of the Lord is the seventh great Day, these signs effectively signal Christ's return in the rapture at the end of this age.

In the revelation given to John on the island of Patmos, Jesus clarified Joel's part of the prophecy by revealing that these celestial signs *would include the stars as well,* not just the sun and moon.

> I looked when He opened the sixth seal, and behold, there was a great earthquake; and the sun became black as sackcloth of hair, and the moon became like blood.
>
> And the stars of heaven fell to the earth as a fig tree drops its late figs when it is shaken by a

mighty wind… for the great Day of His wrath
has come, and who is able to stand?[1]

These and other passages we have studied define the length of
the great tribulation. It began with the abomination of desolation
back in the first century. It will not end until the celestial signs of
darkness signal the advent of the seventh prophetic Day—the great
and awesome Day of the Lord.

Prophetic Facts about the Great Tribulation

We can now clarify some misconceptions about *the great tribulation*. First, the term itself *measures the span of time* attributed to
"the time of Jacob's trouble" or birth pains. It relates to the prophecy
in Hosea 6:1–2 in which the nation of Israel would be "torn and
stricken" for the better part of two great Days, only to be fully healed
and revived on the third prophetic Day. This establishes the length of
time assigned to the great tribulation.

Second, even though all nations have been afflicted during this
time of great and unparalleled tribulation, this prophetic period
relates specifically to the nation of Israel.

From a prophetic standpoint, it is the time of *Jacob's* trouble. It
is a Jewish term. It began with the siege against Jerusalem, the capital
of the Jewish nation. It will come to an end when Israel returns to
the Lord and confesses, "Blessed is He who comes in the name of the
Lord." And even though the whole world has suffered to some extent
or another during this time, the term primarily relates to the people
of Israel and their captivity among the nations.

In Luke's account, Jesus said, *"For these are the days of vengeance,*
[against Israel] *that all things which are written* [against them by the
Jewish prophets] *may be fulfilled."* He continued, *"For there will be
great distress in the land and wrath upon this people."*

---

[1]   Revelation 6:12–13 and 17

Third, the end of the great tribulation marks the start of Israel's third-Day revival and deliverance. Since the celestial signs of darkness will signal the advent of the Day of the Lord, they also signal the arrival of *the third prophetic Day* of Hosea's prophecy.

This explains why *things will actually get worse in the world even though the great tribulation has come to an end*. It is because the Day of the Lord will inaugurate *God's wrath upon the Gentile nations*, especially those within the kingdom of the beast.

So even though things will get worse for the nations, they will get better for the nation of Israel. Her birthing pains will subside with the birth (or revealing) of the "sons of God" in the rapture. Since the coming of the Lord will spark Israel's newfound faith in Christ, as new believers they will be protected from His wrath according to the provisions of the ninety-first Psalm. Therefore, Joel prophesied,

> The sun and moon will grow dark and the stars will diminish their brightness. The Lord will also roar from Zion and utter His voice from Jerusalem.
>
> The heavens and earth will shake [in His wrath], but the Lord will be a shelter for His people and the strength of the children of Israel.

Therefore, even though the great tribulation will come to an end at that time, things will get worse on the earth. The Gentile nations will incur the wrath of God in that Day. Israel, on the other hand, will receive God's blessings of protection and strength.

As far as the *election* (choosing and calling) of their forefathers, those in Israel who get saved *after* the rapture will ultimately stand at the head of the natural nations. As born-again Christians, they will be *kept through* the hour of trial coming upon the whole earth.

In contrast, there is a *heavenly calling* that pertains to the Lord's Church, Body, and Bride according to Hebrews 3:1 and Ephesians 1:18. As *His elect*, we will be *kept from* the hour of trial, not through it.

8

Those Days Will Be Shortened

In Luke 13:32, Jesus indicated that His anointed ministry would continue for two prophetic Days. As the Head of a new Man, He started this ministry when He was about thirty years old, sometime between AD 26 and 30. It has continued ever since through the Church, which is His Body. After two Days, this new Man will be completed.

This means that the Day of the Lord, the third Day of Christ, the seventh Day from Adam, and the last Day of God's great Week, however you choose to say it, will dawn in the next decade sometime between AD 2026 and 2030. *This appears to be all the time that the Church has left on this planet to fulfill our preaching assignment.*

So from the perspective of our generation, the Bible does not teach that the great tribulation is coming *but that the "snare of that Day" is coming.* In Luke's account, Jesus said,

> Be careful, or your hearts will be weighed down
> with dissipation, drunkenness, and the anxieties
> of life, and that Day will close on you unexpect-

edly like a trap; for it will come upon all those
who live on the face of the whole earth.[1]

In the next sentence, He encouraged believers to, therefore,
"watch and pray" so that we might "escape and stand" before the Son
of Man.

In other words, Christ's return in the rapture will provide *a
timely escape* from the snare that will come upon all who remain on
the earth. It will happen just as that Day begins to dawn. In Scripture,
that Day is simply an abbreviated expression for *the Day of the Lord.*

That Day will not come unexpectedly for those who can "see
the Day approaching,"[2] for its approach can be monitored by counting the number of years that have lapsed since the start of Jesus's ministry. For our generation, these two prophetic Days are nearly spent.

The Questions No One Thought to Ask

Knowing that the Olivet Discourse is not about the final years
of the Antichrist puts a whole new slant on Jesus's teaching. It means
that His teaching was directed to those who would be looking for His
return, not those who would be left behind once He comes.

This is the key to understanding the remainder of His teaching,
for the idea of a "second coming" was a mystery *that had been hidden*
from the eyes of men in Old Testament times.

No one anticipated that the long-awaited Messiah would come,
only to be rejected, crucified, and raised from the dead. Nor did anyone anticipate that He would then ascend into heaven, only to return
again after another lengthy wait. And even though these things had
been written, *they were sealed* so that the nation of Israel would have
a legitimate opportunity to embrace Jesus as their Messiah when He
first appeared.

---

[1]   Luke 21:34–36
[2]   Hebrews 10:25

It is, therefore, helpful to consider how much the disciples *didn't know* as they sat with Jesus that day on the Mount. It is obvious that they were still struggling to understand why He had to leave, much less "how" and "when" He would come back.

So the notion of a "second coming" opened up a whole new set of questions—questions that none of them had even thought to ask. For one thing, how would Jesus come back? Would He just suddenly appear somewhere out in the wilderness, or perhaps in the Temple? Would they hear a rumor of His appearance and need to go seek Him?

How long would He be gone? If His absence was long enough, what would happen to the believers who died while He was away? Since He promised to raise the dead at His return, how would that happen?

Even more importantly, if the dead are raised and glorified at His coming, what about the believers that would be living on earth when He returns? *Would they miss out on the regeneration?* Since living believers cannot be raised from the dead, when would they be glorified as their fellow brethren? Would they still reign with Him in spite of their mortal frames?

These were questions that none of His disciples even thought to ask at the time of Jesus's Olivet teaching. Today, we know the answers, but only because we have the New Testament letters written by men like Paul. But where did *they* get the answers?

Jesus knew that these would become important concerns after His departure. So the remainder of Jesus's teaching was geared to not only answer their remaining question about the sign of His coming, *but all the other questions that they didn't even know to ask.*

So as His Discourse continued, He began to teach them about His return. He taught them what it will be like, how it will happen, and just as importantly, how He will gather all those who have believed on Him to Himself—*both the living and the dead.*

Even though Jesus knew that they would not be able to grasp all that He was saying at the time, He also knew that the Holy Spirit would pick up where He left off, by bringing these things back to their remembrance and by helping them to understand all that was said.

In doing so, the Church would have a sure and certain hope for the future. The concept of His coming in the rapture would not only stand upon a rock-solid foundation, but would receive the appropriate status of being "a word from the Lord" as well.

Therefore, the Olivet Discourse marks the first formal teaching on the rapture. It describes how the Son of Man will come to gather His elect in that Day. It answers the questions that no one ever thought to ask.

And even though various elements of the teaching can be traced back to the Old Testament, once we know what to look for, you will not find a clearer and more thorough presentation of the rapture until it was repeated by the apostles in their New Testament letters.

So after telling them about a time of great and unparalleled tribulation, Jesus began to unveil the rapture by saying, *"And unless those days were shortened, no flesh would be saved; but for the elect's sake those days will be shortened."*[3]

Shorten What Days?

We will examine the phrase "unless those days were shortened" more fully in the next chapter. But for now it is important to realize that the *length of time* stated in various prophecies, whether the last half of Daniel's seventieth week or the length of the sixth great Day, will not be "shortened" or altered. Otherwise, the prophecies would have noted the shorter value instead.

So when Jesus said that He would minister for a prophetic *Today* and *Tomorrow*, He meant exactly that. And when Hosea prophesied that Israel would be torn and stricken during two great Days, we were meant to understand the prophecy *as stated.* Such prophecies enable us to anticipate the arrival of the third prophetic Day.

Furthermore, there are at least nine different prophecies that assign a full three and one-half years to the last half of Daniel's seventieth week. We will see what Jesus meant by shortening the days a bit

---

3   Matthew 24:22

later. But for now, realize that *the set length of time stated in prophecies such as these will not change.*

Many have also struggled to understand the phrase "no flesh would be saved." It has been commonly understood to mean "the end of all human life." So if you were taught that the Olivet Discourse is about the final years of the Antichrist, it is only natural to conclude that "unless Jesus intervenes at the battle of Armageddon, the whole world will be destroyed. No flesh will survive."

But once we realize that the same sign that signals *the end* of "the tribulation of those days" also signals *the advent* of the Lord's return in "last-Day resurrection," it becomes clear that Jesus was referring to the rapture at this point in His teaching.

So when Jesus said that no flesh would be "saved," He was referring to the kind of "salvation" that believers will receive in their bodies at the rapture. Luke's account states, "Now when these things begin to happen, look up and lift up your heads, because *your redemption* draws near." Here, Jesus was referring to the glorification of our flesh-and-blood bodies.

Not only that, we will also be "saved" from the wrath to come in that Day. Therefore, in 1 Thessalonians 5:9, Paul wrote, "For God did not appoint us to wrath, but to *obtain salvation* through our Lord Jesus Christ." In 2 Thessalonians 1:10, he exhorted us "to wait for His Son from Heaven… even Jesus, who *delivers us* from the wrath to come." Again, in Romans 8:23, Paul wrote that we are "groaning and waiting for the *redemption* of our body."

In this way, Jesus introduced His disciples to an aspect of His coming that no one had ever anticipated—the truth that the "days of His elect will be shortened" by removing us from this planet. He will do this in order to bring about *the fullness of our salvation* and to *save us from the wrath to come.*

9

For the Sake of His Elect

From here on in the Discourse, Jesus began to teach His disciples about an aspect of His return that no one had ever anticipated. Today, we call it the rapture, but back then, they often called it *the gathering*.

Following His description of the tribulation of those days, Mark's account records Jesus as saying, "And unless the Lord had shortened those days, no flesh would be saved; but for the elect's sake, whom He chose, He shortened the days."

The Greek word translated *shortened* literally means "to cut off or amputate." The word was used in the Greek translation of 2 Samuel 4:12 when David's men *cut off* the hands and feet of the men who murdered Ishbosheth.

The word conveys the idea of the sudden abbreviation or removal of something that would normally have remained.

We know that for the nation of Israel, the tribulation of those days will run their full course—two Days of being torn and stricken until their revival on the third Day. Since this marks the time of Christ's return, we can easily understand how Israel's "days of vengeance" will come to an end even though their appointed length was not shortened in terms of time. Even so, this does not explain how "the days will be cut off for the sake of the elect."

Who Are the Elect?

If you think that the elect refers to the Jews during the final years of the Antichrist, you'll miss much of what Jesus taught throughout His Discourse. In doing so, you'll have to ignore what the New Testament says about *the elect*.

In the Greek New Testament, the word is used as an adjective, a noun, and a verb. As an adjective, *eklektos* means "selected, chosen, and picked out." As a noun, *ekloge* means "that which is chosen." And as a verb, *eklego* means "to choose." Mark's account captures the fuller meaning by writing, "but for the elect's (*eklektos*) sake, whom He has chosen (*eklego*), He shortened the days."

The New Testament epistles were written to believers. These letters leave us no doubt as to the identity of the elect. In Romans 8:32–33, we find,

> He who did not spare His own Son, but delivered Him up for us all, how shall He not with Him also freely give us all things? Who shall bring a charge against God's elect? It is God who justifies.

According to Paul, the elect are those who have been justified by faith in Jesus Christ. To the Colossians, he wrote, "Therefore, as the elect of God, holy and beloved, put on tender mercies, kindness, humility, meekness, longsuffering."[1] In 1 Thessalonians 1:2–4, the elect are his beloved brethren for whom he gave thanks and prayed for continually.

> Remembering without ceasing your work of faith, labor of love, and patience of hope in our Lord Jesus Christ in the sight of our God and Father, knowing, beloved brethren, your election by God.

---

[1] Colossians 3:12

In Romans 11:5–7, the apostle made a distinction between the Jewish believers who have received Christ and the unbelieving nation at large by saying, "Even so then, at this present time there is a remnant according to the election of grace." In verse 7, he concluded, "What then? Israel has not obtained what it seeks, but the elect have obtained it, and the rest were blinded."

The unbelieving nation of Israel is never called the elect under the New Covenant. Instead, it is a term that is reserved for the Church—those who have obtained God's grace by faith. In 1 Peter 1:2, Peter addressed his letter to the believers in Pontus, Galatia, Cappadocia, Asia, and Bithynia, saying,

> Elect according to the foreknowledge of God the Father, in sanctification of the Spirit, for obedience and sprinkling of the blood of Jesus Christ: Grace to you and peace be multiplied.

In his second epistle, Peter wrote to "those who have obtained like precious faith with us," saying, "Therefore, brethren, be even more diligent to make your calling and election sure, for if you do these things you will never stumble."[2]

Mark noted that the elect are "those whom the Lord *has chosen*." Therefore, in John 15:16, Jesus said, "You did not choose Me, but I chose you and appointed you that you should go and bear fruit, and that your fruit should remain, that whatever you ask the Father in My name He may give you." Jesus's statement was not limited to His twelve disciples. His "choosing" refers to every believer, whether Jew or Gentile, who makes up the body of Christ.

Therefore, Peter wrote, "But you are a chosen generation, a royal priesthood, a holy nation, His own special people, that you may proclaim the praises of Him who called you out of darkness into His marvelous light."[3]

---

[2]   2 Peter 1:10

[3]   1 Peter 2:9

Likewise, in Ephesians 1:4, Paul revealed "just as He chose us in Him before the foundation of the world, that we should be holy and without blame before Him in love." Finally, Revelation 17:14 states,

> These will make war with the Lamb, and the Lamb will overcome them, for He is Lord of lords and King of kings; and those who are with Him are called "chosen and faithful."

In light of the New Testament, if you believe on the Lord Jesus Christ, if you have obtained like precious faith with the apostles, then you are justified in God's sight. You are beloved, holy, blameless, called, selected, picked out, and chosen by God. *You are His elect.*

For your sake, the Lord Himself will "shorten the days." He will literally cut them off. Do you see it yet? Let me paraphrase it to make it a bit clearer. *He will cut off the days of the elect for their sake.* Now do you see it?

Since the "cutting off of these days" happens when the celestial signs announce the end of the great tribulation and the advent of that Day, *this links the "shortening of days for the elect's sake" with the coming of the Son of Man!*

In other words, our days on the earth will be cut off, abbreviated; and our lifetimes will be shortened when Jesus comes in the rapture. He will seize you from this planet to join Him in clouds of glory.

When that happens, your days here will end. If you are forty years old when He comes, you will not live to be eighty. Your days will no longer be measured in terms of this earthly realm. Instead, you will be quickened to live with Him in glory forever.

Jesus said that He will do this for *your sake.* Why is that? It is so you can escape the snare of that Day, "the hour of trial that will come upon the whole world."

> Because you have kept My command to persevere, I also will keep you from the hour of trial

which shall come upon the whole world, to test
those who dwell on the earth.[4]

In His great mercy, God will cut short your days on planet
earth and remove you to His Father's house. Therefore, Paul knew to
write, "For God did not appoint us to wrath, but to obtain salvation
through our Lord Jesus Christ."[5]

Once the great tribulation comes to an end, the wrath of *that
Day* will fall upon the nations. It need not fall upon you. If you are
"waiting for His Son from heaven," then Jesus will "deliver you from
the wrath to come."[6]

He will not shorten the days of the great tribulation, nor will
He shorten the remaining years of the Antichrist, *but He will shorten
yours!* He will do this because you are His chosen Bride.

As the elect, we have believed on the Lord even though *we hav-
en't seen Him*. Therefore, our days on the earth will be shortened. He
will "receive us to Himself" when He comes.

Conversely, the unbelieving nation of Israel will also believe on
Him, *but not until after they have seen Him*. Even though they will be
redeemed, and even though their "earthly calling" remains intact on
account of their forefathers, they will have missed out on the "heavenly calling."

I realize that this "take" on the Olivet Discourse may be new to
most, but this is how "men like Paul" understood it. Eventually, the
New Testament apostles realized that Jesus's Olivet teaching introduced a mystery that had never been seen before—how some would
be "taken" and others "left" when He comes in "His Day."

---

4   Revelation 3:10
5   1 Thessalonians 5:9
6   1 Thessalonians 1:10

10

Taken

Jesus revealed the first hint of the rapture when He taught that He would *shorten the days* for the sake of His elect. After His departure, "another Helper" (the Holy Spirit) would come and teach them what that meant.

Jesus continued to expand this revelation for the remainder of His Discourse. By doing so, He answered the questions they didn't think to ask. So in the next segment, He makes it clear *just how He will return.*

> Then if anyone says to you, "Look, here is the Christ!" or "There!" do not believe it. For false christs and false prophets will rise and show great signs and wonders to deceive, if possible, even the elect. Therefore, if they say to you, "Look, He is in the desert!" Do not go out; or "Look, He is in the inner rooms [of the Temple]!" Do not believe it.
>
> For as the lightning comes from the east and flashes to the west, so also will the coming of the

Son of Man be. For wherever the carcass is, there
the eagles will be gathered together.[1]

Jesus was not describing the final years of the Antichrist. He was describing what the Church would see up until the end of this age. Who can deny that the world has seen the rise of false Christs, false prophets, and false religions over the past two millennia?

We have not only witnessed premature announcements as to the time of the Lord's return, but those who have deceived people by proclaiming themselves to be a great prophet or some sort of messianic figure. Sadly, some of these cults resulted in mass suicides. Even more, some of these people were former believers as well.

Jesus made it clear that His return will not be a secret event. It will be as visible and jolting as lightning that flashes across the sky. A few verses later, He makes this point even clearer by noting that He will come on the clouds of heaven with power and great glory.

But before that, Matthew's account interjects the strange statement, "For wherever the carcass is, there the eagles will be gathered together." The Greek word translated *carcass* means "a lifeless body or corpse." It is derived from a word that means "ruined" or "corrupted." What did Jesus mean by this?

Once again, Luke's Gospel provides some valuable insights. His parallel passage actually appears in chapter 17, verses 22–37. It begins with, "Then Jesus said to the disciples,"

> The days will come when you will desire to see
> one of the days of the Son of Man and you will
> not see it. And they will say to you, "Look here!"
> or "Look there!" Do not go after them or follow
> them.
>
> For as the lightning that flashes out of one part
> under heaven shines to the other part under
> heaven, so also the Son of Man will be in His

---

[1] Matthew 24:23–28

Day. But first He must suffer many things and be rejected by this generation.

The fact that Jesus said this to His disciples makes it clear that He was not referring to the Jews during the final years of the Antichrist. He was referring to the time *when believers would long to see the Lord during His absence.*

He warned them not to fall for "false announcements" of His arrival or the notion that His return would be a secretive affair. Instead, they were to expect Him to come as lightning flashing across the sky, an event visible to all below.

Next, Jesus used the examples of Noah's deliverance from the flood and Lot's escape from the destruction of Sodom to teach His disciples about another forthcoming escape—when some would be taken and others left behind.

> I tell you, in that night there will be two in one bed; the one will be taken and the other will be left. Two will be grinding together; the one will be taken and the other left. Two will be in the field; the one will be taken and the other left.

At the time, Jesus's disciples didn't quite understand, so they asked, "Where, Lord?" From the context, "being taken" was the equivalent of "Noah entering the Ark" and "Lot departing from Sodom." They must have been wondering, "Since it will be like Noah and Lot when you come like lightning to deliver us, where will we be taken? For sure, we won't be taken to another Ark, or to a nearby city, so where?" Jesus answered, *"Wherever the body is, there the eagles will be gathered together."*

As we will see, His enigmatic statement contained a great truth about the rapture, one that would be clearly explained later in His teaching.

But before that, there is a valuable revelation to be gained by examining the word *taken.* Our English translations do not bring out the full meaning of the word. Therefore, we don't hear what the disciples heard when Jesus used the word.

In Greek, the word is *paralambano*. Besides its meaning "to receive," it means "to take to" or "with oneself." It was commonly used of "taking or receiving a wife" or of "taking a person or persons along with you."

Jesus used the word in His bridal promise, "And if I go and prepare a place for you, I will come again and receive (*paralambano*) you to Myself, that where I am, there you may be also." Therefore, in the rapture, Jesus will come and *take us* to His Father's house that we may remain with Him from then on.

The word appears again in Matthew 17:1: "Now after six days Jesus took (*paralambano*) Peter, James, and John his brother, led them up on a high mountain by themselves and He was transfigured before them... "

Jesus said and did these things knowing that His disciples would not make all the prophetic connections prior to the cross. This is why He placed so much emphasis on the future ministry of the promised Spirit. The Holy Spirit would bring these things to their remembrance and "lead and guide them into all truth."

Eventually, they would understand that the strange scenario of the "ones taken" and the "ones left" meant that Jesus will come and *receive us to Himself* as His eternal Bride. We will be taken to His Father's house of many mansions, the place specifically prepared for His adoring Bride.

They realized that the time would come when He would take all of His disciples to a future mountain of transfiguration, the heavenly Mount Zion, where "our faces will shine like the sun and our garments become white as the light." There we will hear the Father speak to us corporately, saying, "You are My beloved Son in whom I am well pleased."

As we can see, brick by brick and line upon line, Jesus's teaching began to piece together the rapture. Eventually, His disciples realized that the days of His elect on planet earth will be cut off when He appears like lightning and takes us to be with Him in heaven.

We will be received as a glorious Bride. We will be transfigured to share in His glory. It will happen when the celestial signs signal the end of the great tribulation and the coming of the Day of the Lord, even His Day.

It will be a worldwide event, happening simultaneously all around the world. For some, it will be nighttime, when two are in one bed sleeping. For others, it will be daytime, when two are at work grinding in the mill or at work in the fields.

As far as the calendar and the clock, it will be a different day and a different hour, depending on your particular location on this planet. Either way, our days will be shortened, and our lifetimes here on earth will be cut off.

The disciples wished to know *where* they would be taken. But Jesus had already told them that part. The Spirit would remind them of that later. The question they didn't think to ask was, "By whom will we be taken?"

A Gathering of Eagles

The Greek word for *eagles* is *aetos*. It refers to godly angelic beings. In contrast, the passages in Revelation 19:17 and 21 use the word *orneon* to refer to "all the unclean fowls" or "birds of prey" that will feast on the slain bodies at the battle of Armageddon.

The word *aetos*, or eagle, appears in Revelation 4:7 to describe the fourth living being guarding God's throne—"and the fourth living being was like a flying eagle." It appears again in Revelation 8:13 when John heard an *eagle* (*aetos* in the Greek but translated *angel*) flying through the midst of heaven, saying, "Woe, woe, woe to the inhabitants of the earth."

In Revelation 12:14, the revived nation of Israel (represented by the woman) "was given two wings of a great eagle (*aetos*), that she might fly into the wilderness" to escape the serpent.

In Matthew's account, Jesus said that the eagles will be gathered to where the "dead, ruined, and corrupted bodies" (*ptoma*) can be found. In Luke's account, Jesus said "to where the living and soundly whole bodies" (*soma*) can be found. The Spirit made sure to include both, the dead in Christ, and those that remain.

Either way, whether dead or alive, Jesus is coming to take those who are His at His coming. For those who wait upon the Lord, He will come and exchange His immortal strength for our mortal strength—*so that we might "mount up with wings as eagles!"*

11

The Sign of His Coming

Jesus's disciples asked two questions that day as they sat with Him on the Mount of Olives. Their first question concerned the destruction of their Temple. "What sign will indicate when these things will happen?" The answer was, "When you see the abomination of desolation standing in the holy place, that is, when you see Jerusalem surrounded by armies."

We were also told that this event would trigger a prolonged time of great and unparalleled tribulation. At this point, Jesus began to unveil the rapture. He began with the promise that He would cut short our days upon the earth in order to "save" our fleshly bodies and to deliver us from the wrath to come.

He eliminated the notion that His return would be anything but secret. Instead it would be as eye-catching as the lightning that flashes from the east to the west.

He went on to reveal that when He comes in His Day, some would be taken, while others are left behind. His eagles would be gathered to both the dead and living bodies of His elect so that His Bride may be safely received to His Father's house.

Having laid this foundation, Jesus proceeded to answer their second question, "What will be the sign of your coming and of the end of the age?"

Notice again how the Holy Spirit inspired Matthew to state this question. First, the word for *sign* is singular. This is because there is but one sign, and one sign alone, that qualifies as *the sign of His coming.* Second, the same sign that signals Christ's return *also signals the end of this age.*

As His teaching progresses, it becomes abundantly clear that Jesus not only linked His visible coming with the end of this age *but with the rapture as well.*

This eliminates another false notion widely held in the Church today—the notion that the rapture could happen at any time *and apart from any signs.*

The Celestial Sign of Darkness

Picking up where each Gospel writer left off, Mark's account continues with Jesus saying,

> But in those days, after that tribulation, the sun will be darkened, and the moon will not give its light; the stars of heaven will fall, and the powers in the heavens will be shaken. Then they will see the Son of Man coming in the clouds with great power and glory.

The next verse in Luke's account says,

> And there will be signs in the sun, moon, and stars; and on the earth distress of nations, with perplexity, the sea and the waves roaring; men's hearts failing them from fear and the expectation of those things which are coming on the earth, for the powers of the heavens will be shaken.

> Then they will see the Son of Man coming in a cloud with power and great glory.

Finally, Matthew's account states,

> Immediately after the tribulation of those days the sun will be darkened, and the moon will not give its light; the stars will fall from heaven, and the powers of the heavens will be shaken. Then the sign of the Son of Man will appear in heaven, and then all the tribes of the earth will mourn, and they will see the Son of Man coming on the clouds of heaven with power and great glory.

Notice that each account begins this segment with certain "signs" appearing in the sun, moon, and stars. Next, each account mentions the "visible coming of the Son of Man in power and glory." Since it was Jesus's intent to answer their question, whatever we just read prior to "His coming" must be "the sign of His coming."

These celestial signs are also linked with God "shaking the powers of the heavens." As God begins to shake "these powers," the cumulative effect is that all heavenly light over this planet will be diminished. In effect, God will turn off the lights.

The sun is darkened, the moon refuses to shine, and the stars appear to fall and burn out. Without sunlight, moonlight, or starlight, the heavens above the entire earth will become dark. *This all-encompassing darkness is the sign of His coming.*

Isaiah prophesied, "Arise, shine, for your light has come, and the glory of the Lord rises upon you. See, darkness covers the earth and thick darkness is over the peoples, but the Lord rises upon you and His glory appears over you."[1] With gross darkness enveloping the whole earth, the stage is set for all to be blinded by the sudden appearance of His glory. He will shine like lightning.

---

[1]   Isaiah 60:1–2 (NIV)

As He descends with the shout of the Bridegroom, His first command will cause the dead to be raised. Therefore, He will shout, "Arise!" to the bodies of the dead in Christ. His second command will cause the mortal bodies of living believers to be changed. Therefore, He will command the rest of us to "shine!" In an instant, we will be clothed with immortality.

Shaking Heaven and Earth

In Luke's account, the signs in the sun, moon, and stars follow the "days of vengeance," the time of Israel's captivity among the nations. In Mark's account, these celestial signs of darkness occur "after that tribulation." Matthew's account is even more explicit, for he wrote that these signs would be observed "immediately after the tribulation of those days."

Collectively, these celestial signs form the "sign" of His coming and the end of this age. In Greek, the word for *sign* is *semeion*, meaning "an indication." Therefore, the darkening of the sun, moon, and stars *together* will indicate that the time of His coming is at hand.

All three Gospel accounts concur: this sign will appear as God shakes the powers in the heavens above us. Along these lines, the passage in Hebrews 12:26 states,

> But now He has promised, saying, "Yet once more
> I shake not only the earth, but also the heaven."

Together, these celestial signs form "the sign" that announces His coming. They are specifically mentioned at least nine times in Scripture. Invariably, they are connected with the prophetic theme of God shaking the powers of the heavens and the coming of the Day of the Lord. For example, Joel 3:14–16 states,

> Multitudes, multitudes in the valley of decision!
> For the Day of the Lord is near in the valley of
> decision. The sun and moon will grow dark, and
> the stars will diminish their brightness.

> The Lord also will roar from Zion and utter His voice from Jerusalem; the heavens and earth will shake; but the Lord will be a shelter for His people and the strength of the children of Israel.

These same themes are repeated again in other passages, such as Isaiah 13:9–13.

> Behold, the Day of the Lord comes, cruel, with both wrath and fierce anger to lay the land desolate; and He will destroy its sinners from it. For the stars of heaven and their constellations will not give their light; the sun will be darkened in its going forth, and the moon will not cause its light to shine.

> I will punish the world for its evil… therefore, I will shake the heavens and the earth will move out of her place in the wrath of the Lord of hosts and in the Day of His fierce anger.

Unlike solar and lunar eclipses that have occurred periodically at various times in the past, this "sign of darkness" will be attributable to the darkening of the sun, moon, and stars *simultaneously*. As a result, the entire heavens will grow dark. Psalm 82:5 says,

> They do not know, nor understand; they walk about in darkness. All the foundations of the earth are unstable.

Signs or Wonders?

The truth that these celestial signs will not appear until God shakes the heavens differentiates them from the regular cycles of solar and lunar eclipses that have occurred at various times in conjunction with Jewish feasts.

Even though past occurrences of solar eclipses and "blood moons" *were very important omens,* we should not confuse them with the sign of darkness that Jesus referred to in His Olivet Discourse.

For one thing, nothing happened to the stars during such eclipses. Nor were all heavenly lights darkened together all at once. Furthermore, these eclipses *did not signal the end of the great tribulation.*

We need to ask ourselves, "Did the tribulation of those days immediately end when any of these blood-moon eclipses appeared? Did the heavens shake? Did the stars appear to be falling from the night sky? Did the heavens above grow completely dark all over the world?"

Does this mean that blood-moons and solar eclipses have no relevance to prophecy? No, not at all, for they serve an important prophetic purpose in warning people *that His coming is getting closer.* In contrast, the singular sign of darkness will tell us *that His coming is at hand.*

The phenomenon known as "blood-moons" can be found in a prophecy from Joel. Peter quoted this strategic prophecy on the Day of Pentecost. It appears in the second chapter of Acts. Verse 19 states,

> And I will show wonders in heaven above and
> signs in the earth beneath.

The Greek word translated *wonders* is *tarata,* the plural form of *taras.* It means "an omen or a wonder." Since Peter was quoting the prophet Joel, the corresponding Hebrew word is *mopheth,* meaning, "something conspicuous, a token, or an omen."

The "wonders in heaven above" refers to the uncanny connections we have observed between solar and lunar eclipses, Jewish feast days, and the fulfillment of important events with respect to Israel. As omens or harbingers, they tell us that we are *getting closer and closer* to Christ's return.

In contrast, the singular sign of darkness in the sun, moon, and stars will *signal the advent of the Day of the Lord.* This sign appears in the next verse of Joel's prophecy.

> The sun shall be turned into darkness and the moon into blood before the coming of the great and awesome Day of the Lord.

It is also featured in the following passage from Revelation 6:12–17 as the sixth seal is opened:

> I looked when He opened the sixth seal, and behold, there was a great earthquake; and the sun became black as sackcloth of hair; and the moon became like blood.

> And the stars of heaven fell to the earth, as a fig tree drops its late figs when it is shaken by a mighty wind.

> Then the sky receded as a scroll when it is rolled up, and every mountain and island was moved out of its place.

The passage continues by describing how unbelievers from all around the world will be suddenly stricken with fear and panic, saying, "Hide us from the face of Him who sits on the throne and from the wrath of the Lamb—for the great Day of His wrath has come!"

We will look at the seven seals found in the book of Revelation later. For now, we need to see the difference between *the omens* and *the sign.* Blood moons and solar eclipses are important, for they tell us that the Lord's return *is very near.* The sign of darkness, on the other hand, tells us that the great Day of His wrath *has come.*

As this heavenly alarm sounds all around the world, those who have ears to hear will know that it is time "to arise and shine!"

12

Gathered by Angels

Jesus concluded His age-ending scenario of events by informing His disciples of what would happen once the world sees Him coming in the clouds. Mark's account continues by saying,

> And then He will send His angels, and gather together His elect from the four winds, from the farthest part of earth to the farthest part of heaven.

Matthew's account is very similar with the noted exception that the angels will be sent forth with "the great sound of a trumpet."

> And He will send His angels with a great sound of a trumpet, and they will gather together His elect from the four winds, from one end of heaven to the other.

There are those who would teach that this "gathering" refers to a time after the battle of Armageddon when God will gather the Jewish people back to Israel.

If that were so, why would God need to send His angels to do the gathering? Can't the Jewish people make the trip themselves? And why would they need to be gathered "from one end of heaven to the other"? Isn't that what jets are for? No one needs the "sound of a great trumpet" to hop on a jet and fly to Israel.

Obviously, I am being sarcastic, and I certainly mean no offense to the Jewish people. I simply wish to show how "uninspired" some of our interpretations of the Olivet Discourse have been.

Up to this point, Jesus has not said anything about the battle of Armageddon. Yet we assumed that the battle must have taken place merely because the visible coming of the Son of Man in the Day of the Lord was depicted in the previous verse.

Today, most people would not link that verse with the rapture, for the notion that the Olivet Discourse is all about the final years of the Antichrist runs very deep in the Church today. Most would not even acknowledge that the rapture *is the second coming of Christ.*

For those who think that Jesus was teaching about the final years leading up to Armageddon, isn't it strange that Jesus said nothing about the Antichrist, the mark of the beast, or the worship of his image? Wouldn't these things deserve at least a byline somewhere in His discourse?

On the other hand, if these events are properly assigned to the first few years of the age to come, *then Jesus was right not to include them in His age-ending scenario.*

Even more, since His teaching actually represents a formal unveiling of the rapture, then the absence of these events can only mean *that His elect will not be here to see them!*

The Third Witness

As I said toward the beginning of this book, whenever we find things in the accounts of Matthew and Mark that might not be readily apparent, just turn to see what Luke's account says about it. Luke's account makes it perfectly clear that the "gathering of the elect" is nothing less than the rapture of the Church.

At the precise point in the narrative where Matthew and Mark refer to the gathering of Christ's elect, Luke inserts instead,

> Then they will see the Son of Man coming in a cloud with power and great glory. Now when these things begin to happen, look up and lift up your heads, because your redemption draws near.[1]

The phrase "your redemption" does not refer to a Jewish victory at the battle of Armageddon, but to the completed redemption of believers when Jesus returns and we receive our glorified bodies. The phrase "His elect" refers to His Church, Body, and Bride, just as it did a few verses earlier in His Discourse.

So rather than repeat the statements that the Lord will send out His angels and gather us, Luke's account essentially tells us to "look up and expect to be gathered!"

Luke's third witness keeps us honest. *The gathering of Christ's elect from the four winds can only be the rapture—when we look up and receive the redemption of our bodies.*

It is amazing to realize just how much Jesus revealed about the rapture once we truly behold His teaching in its proper light. He told us how it will happen, when it will happen, and why it will happen.

Much of what the New Testament apostles eventually learned about the rapture came from this critical teaching. If not here, where then did they get it?

Even though the Old Testament contains obscure types and shadows of this glorious gathering, I seriously doubt that anyone would have imagined such an unusual event apart from what Jesus revealed in this teaching.

For instance, how did Paul know that the Lord will descend from heaven "with a shout, with the voice of an archangel, and with the trumpet of God"? How did he know that living believers will be "caught up" when the dead are "raised up"?

---

[1]   Luke 21:27–28

Paul's description of the rapture contains the same markings that Jesus used in describing the gathering of His elect. His descent will be accompanied by an angelic presence and heralded by the sound of the trumpet of God.

Paul also knew that this triumphant gathering would include those "from the farthest parts of heaven to the farthest parts of the earth." So in 1 Thessalonians 4:13–14, he wrote,

> But I do not want you to be ignorant, breth-ren, concerning those who have fallen asleep [in death], lest you sorrow as others who have no hope.

> For if we believe that Jesus died and rose again, even so God will bring with Him those who sleep in Jesus.

As far as believers are concerned, the New Testament teaches that "to be absent from the body is to be present with the Lord."[2] Since part of the Church is already present with the Lord in heaven, Jesus was the first to reveal that this holy gathering will involve *both heaven and earth.*

Therefore, the ancient prophecy of Enoch is quoted in Jude 14 as saying, "Behold, the Lord comes with ten thousands of His saints." Many who have read this have tried to make a distinction between the Lord coming "with His saints" versus coming "for His saints."

Thanks to the Olivet Discourse, we can understand that these are not two separate and distinct events. Jesus will not descend from heaven all by Himself. He is coming with both saints and angels. He will not only come *with His saints* as noted above but *for His saints* down below as well. His saints will be gathered from both heaven and earth.

The apostle Paul was also acutely aware of the word that Jesus used to describe what we now call the rapture. In his second letter

---

2   2 Corinthians 5:1–8

to the Thessalonians, he referred to this event as "the coming of our Lord Jesus Christ *and our gathering together* to Him."[3]

This is the same word that Jesus used in His Olivet teaching. The word is *episunago*. It means "to collect upon the same place" or "gather together."

Is it just a coincidence that Paul used *this same word* when he wrote about our "gathering together" to the Thessalonians? He knew that Jesus was talking about the Church, not the Jewish survivors of Armageddon.

Since Jesus connected this gathering with the age-ending Day of the Lord, Paul also understood when this gathering would take place. In Ephesians 1:10, he wrote, "That in the dispensation of the fullness of the times He might *gather together* in one all things in Christ, *both which are in heaven and which are on earth.*"

When Jesus comes, He will gather all the "things" *that belong to Him*—the decomposed bodies of previously departed saints, their redeemed spirits, the spirits of those of us still living on planet earth, and our "shiny" new bodies.

He will collect these things from the farthest parts of heaven to the farthest parts of the earth. No matter where they are, His angels will seek them out and find them. According to Hebrews 12:22, there is an innumerable company of them to carry out this holy errand.

As you can see, we miss a lot when we misinterpret Jesus's witness on the Mount of Olives. We miss the initial revelation that the lives of living believers will be shortened in order to escape the snare of that Day; that our days will be cut off by being "taken and received" unto the Lord; that we will be gathered by His holy angels; and that, just as importantly, we miss the truth that one day "the eagles" will be gathered to our dead and living bodies.

When Jesus comes, you will not have to make the trip to meet Him alone. He loves you too much for that. Instead, you will be personally gathered by His angels.

---

3   2 Thessalonians 2:1

13

———— ⋈ ————

With Wings as Eagles

As previously noted, Jesus introduced His disciples to an aspect of His coming that no one had ever heard of before—the truth that some will be taken while others are left behind when He comes. Hearing this, His disciples asked, "Where, Lord?" In Luke's account, Jesus responded,

> Wherever the body (*soma*, or living body) is,
> there the eagles will be gathered together.

The Holy Spirit influenced Luke to write it that way so that we would get the full revelation, for Matthew recorded it a bit differently.

> Wherever the carcass (*ptoma*, or lifeless body) is,
> there the eagles will be gathered.

When both statements are read together, we can understand that the eagles will be gathered *to both* the living bodies of believers as well as the lifeless bodies of departed saints. But how did this answer the disciple's question? They asked "where," not "who."

A good teacher knows to ask the right questions in order to lead his students on the path of discovery. Asking the *right* question will enable them to see things they didn't even think to ask. In this case, *the real question* was "who," not just "where." Once you understand "who will do the gathering," the answer to the question of *where* becomes obviously apparent.

Later, Jesus clarified the truth that His angels will do the gathering by saying, "And the Son of Man will send His angels with a great sound of a trumpet, and *they* will gather together His elect from the four winds." But this raises a question: why didn't He say "angels" the first time? Why did He say "eagles" instead?

What other truth did He want us to see besides the idea that we will be gathered by angels? Was there something about eagles in the Old Testament that He wanted us to connect with the rapture?

Apparently there was, and who else but Paul and Luke to pick up on it. This becomes evident when we consider that Luke's account makes another "worthy" contribution by adding something not found in the accounts of Matthew and Mark. Where their accounts end, Luke's continues by saying,

> But take heed to yourselves, lest your hearts be weighed down with carousing, drunkenness, and cares of this life; and that Day come on you unexpectedly; for it will come as a snare on all those who dwell on the face of the whole earth.
>
> Watch therefore, and pray always that you may be counted worthy to escape all these things that will come to pass and to stand before the Son of Man.

First, it is important to note that Luke's account connects "our time to look up" with the coming of *that Day*, when every eye will see the Lord descend with power and great glory. Therefore, in 2 Thessalonians 2:1–3, the Holy Spirit warned us not to be deceived *by disconnecting* "the coming of our Lord Jesus Christ and our gathering together to Him" from the coming of "the Day of Christ."

This means that the rapture will not be a secret event, nor will it be devoid of any signs as is often taught. So that's the first thing. But there's more. It only becomes apparent, though, when we delve into the Greek words that Luke employed in the passage above.

Expect Overcoming Strength

To begin with, the word for *pray* is *deomai*. The word does not necessarily refer to a formal prayer request but can also mean "to earnestly desire" or "long for." This "*deomai*-prayer" is an earnest longing or desire within our hearts for Jesus to come. This part of the passage could be translated as "always desiring" or "keep desiring."

The part about being "counted worthy" needs some clarification as well, for it actually refers to "receiving His strength," not a "worthiness that we can earn."

The New Testament clearly teaches that we are saved by grace through faith. Every blessing and inherited promise comes to us because He exchanged *His worthiness* for *our unworthiness* on the cross.

Since the promise to "escape and stand" is just one aspect of the "package of salvation," this promise belongs *to anyone and everyone who believes on the Lord Jesus Christ*. In short, our faith in His blood qualifies all of us to receive this promise. It is not based on our past, present, or future works, but on His finished work!

The Greek literally reads, "So that you *may be able* to escape." The *Berkeley Version* says, "So that you *may have ability* to escape." In my view, the *Amplified Bible* says it best, "So that you *may have the full strength and ability*" to escape and stand.

In Greek, this ability or strength is the word *katischuo*. It means "to be thoroughly strong" or "to thoroughly prevail." In the book of Revelation, it links with the phrase "those who overcome." It refers to Christ's believing Church who will overcome death through the prevailing power of resurrection, just as Jesus overcame to sit at His Father's right hand.[1]

So in essence, Jesus said, "Be attentive; set your desire on receiving the prevailing resurrection-strength to escape all these things." This same thought is expressed in Hebrews 9:28: "To those who eagerly wait for Him, He will appear a second time, apart from sin, for salvation."

But how does our earnest desire to receive this prevailing strength relate to eagles?

Strength to Those Who Wait

A prophecy in the book of Isaiah links our earnest desire to receive His prevailing strength with the notion of "mounting up with wings as eagles."

> Have you not known? Have you not heard? The everlasting God, the Lord, the Creator of the ends of the earth neither faints nor is weary. His understanding is unsearchable. He gives power to the weak, and to those who have no might He increases strength.[2]

In the Hebrew language, the words translated *power, might,* and *strength* can also mean "vigor, force, capacity, the means and the ability." They convey the same thought that Jesus conveyed when He spoke of *katischuo,* the prevailing strength needed to escape and stand in His presence.

Isaiah prophesied about the time when the One who never faints or grows weary will pass on *His immortal strength* to those who are weak (who remain in their mortal bodies) and to those who have no strength at all (the bodies of departed believers).

---

[1]   Revelation 3:21
[2]   Isaiah 40:28–29

Those of us who are weak will receive the means and ability to be clothed with His immortal strength. For those bodies that are dead, He will increase "powerfulness and abundant strength."

The passage continues that "even the youths shall faint and be weary, and the young men shall utterly fall, but those who wait on the Lord shall renew their strength. *They shall mount up with wings like eagles.* They shall run and not be weary; they shall walk and not faint."

Although we have commonly read this passage as a promise of fortitude to "soar above life's problems," Isaiah was actually prophesying about the rapture. The prophecy reveals how our mortal weaknesses will be exchanged for an immortal strength that never faints.

The word *renewed* in our English translations does not fully capture the thought being expressed in the Hebrew. It literally means to "hasten away, slide by, pass on, and be altered or changed." *Young's Literal Translation* reads, "But those expecting Jehovah *pass to power.*

Isaiah prophesied that our mortal weaknesses will *hasten away.* We will be changed. In an instant of time, we will receive an impartation of His "ability, capacity, strength, and might."

Paul understood this. He made the connection between being gathered by angels *and the eagles gathering to the bodies of the elect.* Therefore, he wrote the following so that a great mystery could be "passed on" to others:

> Behold, I tell you a mystery: We shall not all sleep, but we shall all be changed—in a moment, in the twinkling of an eye, at the last trumpet. For the trumpet will sound and the dead will be raised incorruptible, and we shall be changed.[3]

Who will be counted worthy to receive this kind of impartation? Isaiah provides the answer, "those who wait upon the Lord." To "wait" means "to confidently expect, to look patiently for, and to bind your desires upon His promise of exchanged strength."

---

[3]   1 Corinthians 15:51–52

Jesus mentioned the angels so that we would be sure to understand "who would do the gathering." He spoke of eagles so that we would be sure to connect with Isaiah's great prophecy and "expect this overcoming strength" when we are gathered.

14

Enoch, Elijah, and Chariots of Fire

Jesus revealed a lot of things about the rapture in His Olivet Discourse. He revealed how the days of the elect will be shortened and cut off to escape the snare of that Day. He revealed how His elect will be taken and received when He comes, how the eagles will be gathered to our living and dead bodies, and that He will send forth His angels to gather us from both heaven and earth.

Because of His teaching, our eyes are now opened to see various allusions to the rapture in the Old Testament. These "types and shadows" not only confirm all of the truths that Jesus taught but provide additional insights as well.

Enoch's Translation

The passage in Genesis 5:23–24 is brief but loaded with insights. It says, "So all the days of Enoch were three hundred and sixty-five years. And Enoch walked with God; and he was not, for God took him."

Enoch is a type of those of us whose days on the earth will be shortened. While many of the other early patriarchs lived much longer, men such as Adam (930 years) and Methuselah (969 years), Enoch's lifetime was shortened to a mere 365 years. His days on the earth were cut off, for God *took him.*

Since he was not the only one in their time to "walk with God," why did God decide to suddenly take him in such an unusual way? Did He want us to ponder a time in the future when those of us who also walk with God will suddenly be taken to shorten our days on the earth?

A parallel passage in Hebrews 11:5 is worth pondering, for it says,

> By faith Enoch was taken away so that he did not see death, "and was not found, because God had taken him;" for before he was taken he had this testimony, that he pleased God.

Enoch was transported to heaven because he had God-pleasing faith. He never experienced death. God took him, and his days were cut off. According to Jesus, *God will do it again* but on a much grander scale!

Elijah and the Chariot of Fire

We don't know *how* Enoch was taken, but we do in the case of Elijah.

> Then it happened, as they continued on and talked, that suddenly a chariot of fire appeared with horses of fire, and separated the two of them; and Elijah went up in a whirlwind into heaven. And Elisha saw it, and cried out, "My father, my father, the chariot of Israel and its horsemen!" So he saw him no more.[1]

---

[1]   2 Kings 2:11–12

Even though Elijah was nearing the end of his days, God didn't wait for him to die. He decided to take him up to heaven in a whirlwind instead. Since God always has a purpose in what He does, it would seem that He wants us to glean some valuable insights about the rapture from this incident as well.

Apparently, we will not just disappear or shoot up in the air like bottle rockets when the rapture happens. Quite the contrary, for Jesus promised that He will send out His angels to personally gather and escort us into His Presence. Like Elijah, we will be gathered by angelic charioteers in royal chariots of fire. We could call it God's limousine service!

Isaiah 66:15 says that the Lord will come with fire "and *with chariots, like a whirlwind…*" This Spirit-empowered wind will resurrect, change, and transport us in the "chariots of God." If Elijah was worthy of such a chariot, are not God's blood-bought saints worthy of such heavenly transport as well?

I gather that each one of us will have our own chariot and angelic charioteer. If you're concerned whether there will be enough chariots to go around, you need not worry. Psalm 68:17 tells us that "the chariots of God are tens of thousands, and thousands of thousands."

And while we're on the subject, did you know that Elijah was not surprised when his chariot appeared? In fact, He knew that it was coming that very day. And if you really want to disturb your end-time theology, others knew it too!

Knowing the Day

The second chapter of second Kings describes the day "when the Lord was about to take up Elijah into heaven by a whirlwind." Throughout that day, his faithful servant Elisha refused to leave his side. Elisha also knew that this was the day, and he was not about to let his master out of his sight until the time of his departure. In fact, he saw him go up!

So when Elijah said that he was going to Bethel, Elisha said, "Then I'm going too." The chapter continues that upon arriving in Bethel,

> The sons of the prophets who were at Bethel came out to Elisha, and said to him, "Do you know that the Lord will take away your master from over you today?" And he said, "Yes, I know, keep silent."

Bethel, by the way, means "House of God." Next, Elijah decided to depart from Bethel to the city of Jericho. So Elisha repacked his suitcase.

Upon arriving at Jericho, the sons of the prophets who were at Jericho came to Elisha and said, "Do you know that the Lord will take away your master from over you today?" And he said, "Yes, I know, keep silent." In the Hebrew language, *Jericho* means "a fragrance carried by the wind."

From Jericho, Elijah was led to go down to the Jordan River. *Jordan* means "to descend" in Hebrew. His chariot of fire appeared once they had crossed the river on dry ground.

Therefore, the shadow cast by this ancient account suggests the following message: When that Day comes, Jesus will descend (Jordan) to escort His household (Bethel) exhibiting the windblown fragrance of desire (Jericho) to heaven in chariots of fire.

Wind is often a type of the Holy Spirit. This fragrant desire permeates heaven whenever the Spirit and the Bride say, "Even so, come, Lord Jesus."

But there is another important truth to glean before leaving this story: Everyone in the account knew that this was the day! Elijah knew it, his servant Elisha knew it, and all the sons of the prophets knew it as well.

Now here's the question: Why did God give us an account of a prophet ascending to heaven in a chariot of fire with such a deliberate emphasis on the fact *that they all knew the day?* Ascending to heaven in a fiery chariot made for a fine story in and of itself. The fact that they all knew when it would happen adds something that we were not expecting, even if they were. It is a significant part of the story.

Could it be that this incident forms a prophetic end-time shadow that our generation was also meant to ponder? Could it be that God is saying, "Your generation can know the Day, just like they knew the day?"

According to Jesus's Olivet scenario, that Day need not come upon anyone by surprise. He said, "Take heed to yourselves... lest that Day come on you unexpectedly."

He exhorted us to "watch" and observe the fig-tree signs so that we could know when "summer is near, even at the door." He explained the sign of His coming and told us "now when these things begin to happen, look up and lift up your heads, because your redemption draws near."

Like Elijah, Elisha, and the sons of the prophets, we too can know the Day. If we don't, it will be our fault, not His.

Those who think that this means setting a calendar date for Christ's return should read the first book in this series, *See the Day Approaching*. It explains what Jesus meant by the day and hour known only to the Father and how it connects to the passing away of heaven and earth.

Most importantly, it explains why Jesus said His coming *would be like the days of Noah*, not the unperceived time of future glory in a new heavens and a new earth.

Incidentally, Noah knew that the flood was coming in his lifetime and upon his generation. In Hebrews 11:7, we find, "By faith Noah, being divinely warned of things not yet seen, moved with godly fear, and prepared an ark for the saving of his household." We won't need an ark when Jesus returns, but we will need to have a chariot reserved for that Day.

So how do we reserve our personal chariot of fire? Just do what Noah did. First, the Bible says that "Noah found grace in the eyes of the Lord."[2] That grace is embodied in the person of Jesus Christ. Find Him, and you will have found grace in the eyes of the Lord.

---

[2]   Genesis 6:8

Second, once Noah found grace, he built the ark. But how does one build a chariot of fire? As we will see, you build it with desire.

15

The Dance of the Two Camps

All three Gospel accounts include Jesus's parable of the fig tree immediately following the angelic gathering of His elect to heaven.

> Now learn this parable from the fig tree: When its branch has already become tender and puts forth leaves, you know that summer is near. So you also, when you see all these things, know that it is near—at the doors![1]

This was no arbitrary choice on His part. He was directing us to the following passage in the Song of Solomon:

> Rise up, my love, my fair one, and come away; for lo, the winter is past, the [spring] rains are over and gone. The flowers appear on the earth… the fig tree puts forth her green figs, and the vines with the tender grapes give a good smell. Rise up, my love, my fair one, and come away!

---

[1]   Matthew 24:32–33

The Song of Solomon appears in the Old Testament. Its actual title is *Solomon's Song of Songs*, as in the greatest love song ever written. It is written as a dialogue between the Beloved, a Shulamite Maiden, and the Daughters of Jerusalem.

The *NIV Study Bible* provides a very interesting footnote concerning the Beloved's maiden, for the word translated *Shulamite* is a feminine form of the name "Solomon," meaning "Solomon's girl!"

Since King Solomon is speaking as "the beloved" throughout the song, he typifies Jesus as both Bridegroom and King. It is also clear that this Shulamite depicts the bride of Christ—the royal "girl" spoken for by the King. As believers, we are *Solomon's girl.*

Therefore, this prophetic love song depicts the intimacy between Christ and His Church *at the end of this age.* No doubt, this explains why Jesus pointed us to this book in His Olivet Discourse. It is not surprising then to find allusions to His return in the rapture throughout the Song.

The sixth chapter begins with the Daughters of Jerusalem asking, "Where has your Beloved gone, O fairest among women?" The Shulamite responds that he has gone to his garden (a type of God's paradise in heaven).

Verses 11–13 connect with Jesus's parable of the fig tree and the Beloved's call for His fair one to "rise up and come away." The Shulamite recounts,

> I went down to see the nut garden, to see the green plants of the valley; to see whether the vines already had budded, and the pomegranates had put forth their bloom. Ere I was aware, my soul's fancy seated me in a princely chariot of my people. (*Berkeley Version*)

Jesus predicted that our end-time observation of the budding fig tree would yield a "knowing" that His return was right at the door. And as with the Shulamite above, many today are being compelled to "go down to the valley to see whether the vines are budding."

The Shulamite's timely awareness that the vines were all in bloom led to a most extraordinary event. The *NIV Study Bible* states, "Before I realized it, my desire set me among the royal chariots of my people." The *New King James Bible* reads, "Before I was even aware, my soul made me as the chariots of my noble people."

One moment she was walking in the valley; and "before she realized it," or "before she was even aware," she was in a chariot! It reminds us of Paul's mysterious statement about being changed in a moment and in the twinkling of an eye. Solomon's girl may have entered that valley on foot, but she left that "valley" behind in a princely chariot of fire!

My Soul's Fancy

Note how she gained access to the chariot. *The New King James* says, "*My soul had made me* as the chariots of my noble people." The *NIV Study Bible* renders it, "*My desire set me among* the royal chariots of my people." The *Berkeley Version* poetically says, "*My soul's fancy seated me in* a princely chariot of my people."

The peculiar idea that her soul, her desire, or her soul's fancy were responsible for her sudden appearance in the chariot explains why scholars call this the most obscure verse in the Song. The paradox is that her desire caused her to be placed in this chariot before "she was even aware"!

By now we should be able to comprehend why the Holy Spirit chose these exact words, for Jesus taught us to earnestly desire the prevailing strength to escape the snare of that Day. Solomon's prophetic Song confirms how *that desire* will cause your chariot of fire to appear.

Notice that the idea is to escape, not endure. A fiery chariot is not necessary if you're going to "stay in the valley and endure." Such chariots are quite handy, though, when it comes time to exit the valley altogether and "stand before the Son of Man" in heaven.

The Dance of the Mahanaim

As the Shulamite departs in her royal chariot, the passage continues with the Daughters of Jerusalem exclaiming,

> Return, return, O Shulamite; return, return, that
> we may look upon you.

As the King descends, these "Daughters of Jerusalem" will finally recognize this lowly Shulamite as being the Messiah's special love. Isaiah prophesied, "The glory of the Lord shall be revealed, and all flesh shall see it together." (This is the same chapter that ends with "mounting up with wings as eagles.)

Their persistent calls for her to return or turn around so that she might be gazed upon elicit the following response from the Shulamite:

> Why would you gaze on the Shulamite? What is
> it you wish to see?

The Daughters reply,

> We want to see the dance of the Mahanaim!

The Hebrew word *mahanaim* (pronounced mak-han-eh) means "two hosts" or "two camps." It comes from Genesis 32:1–2:

> So Jacob went on his way, and the angels of God
> met him. When Jacob saw them, he said, "This
> is God's camp." And he called the name of that
> place Mahanaim (the double camp).

A "double camp" occurs whenever God's camp joins our camp—whenever we are gathered together in one place. This chariot ride will not be a sober affair. We will be filled with joy unspeakable and full of glory! Both camps will dance with all *His might*. Both will be overwhelmed with this glory, for the psalmist wrote,

> You will show me the path of life; in Your presence is fullness of joy; at your right hand are pleasures forevermore.[2]

The glorious sight of Solomon's girl dancing and rejoicing with the angels of God will spark Israel's third-Day revival. They will react like Elisha when he saw Elijah being caught up in a whirlwind.

> And Elisha saw it, and cried out, "My father, my father, the chariot of Israel and its horsemen!"

We have been taught that the rapture will be a secret affair and that believers will just suddenly disappear without a trace. Yet the shadows say otherwise. Elisha saw the chariot of fire. He watched as his mentor was caught up in a whirlwind.

Likewise, the daughters of Jerusalem saw Solomon's girl go up in a royal chariot. Like Elisha, they were enthralled by the spectacle of the "dance of the two camps."

Jesus Himself taught that all the tribes of the earth will see the Son of Man coming on the clouds of heaven with power and great glory. Some will see and mourn. Others, such as "the daughters of Jerusalem," *will see and believe*. It is only logical to conclude that if they see Him coming, *they will also see us leaving*.

In the next section, we will see that Christ's visible return in the rapture will not convince all to believe. Many will remain deceived. If this seems problematic to some, just remember that Lucifer was once an archangel. He was with God in heaven. He beheld God's glory up close and personal. Yet he rebelled and exalted himself against Almighty God to become what he is today.

---

[2]   Psalm 16:11

The Scriptures declare that every eye will see the Lord when He comes. It is time to discard the notion of a secret, any-moment, and signless rapture.

SECTION 2

The Witness from God's Throne

16

The End of this Age Is upon Us

In His Olivet teaching, Jesus revealed the things that the Church would see leading up to the end of this age. He spoke of birth pains, persecution, and how we would preach the Gospel to all nations in spite of great tribulation.

His teaching did not extend beyond the end of this present age for the simple reason that His comments were directed specifically to the Church as His elect.

Since His chosen Bride would be caught up to heaven as the last half of Daniel's seventieth week begins, there was no need to mention anything about the Antichrist, the mark of the beast, or any other event that would occur during the final years leading up to Armageddon.

These events all pertained to the age to come—when Christ's millennial reign would begin, and when the last half of Daniel's seventieth week would resume after being paused for nearly two thousand years.

We found that God's decision to give us three separate accounts of the same teaching was extremely helpful. The subtle variations between these accounts provided a Spirit-inspired commentary on Jesus's teaching.

And while the Lord was faithful to answer the two questions posed by His disciples, He also answered questions they never thought to ask. In doing so, He not only introduced us to various aspects of the rapture but directed us to search it out in the Old Testament Scriptures as well. Our search not only confirmed what He taught but provided other rich insights to round out the revelation.

Among the many highlights of His teaching, He provided an orderly sequence of the major prophetic events associated with this age.

1. The *abomination of desolation*, or siege of Jerusalem, resulting in the destruction of the Jewish Temple, the start of Jacob's birth pains, and the scattering of Israel among the nations;
2. A prolonged time of *great tribulation*; immediately followed by
3. *The celestial sign* of darkness in the sun, moon, and stars as the heavens begin to shake;
4. *The coming of the Son of Man* in power and glory as the tribes of the earth mourn, and as believers look up,
5. And *the gathering* of His elect from the four winds by the angelic host.

Since this teaching took place prior to the cross, all of these events still remained in their future. And even though the Church suffered persecution right from the onset, the Jewish Temple would not be destroyed until nearly forty years later.

It is important to note that prior to the Temple's destruction in AD 70, most of the books that appear in the New Testament were already written and in circulation, including all four Gospel accounts. The most notable exception was the book of Revelation. It was written in the latter part of John's life during his exile on the island of Patmos, probably around AD 95.

Therefore, by the time that John received the visions that form the book of Revelation, certain prophetic events in Jesus's Olivet Discourse *had already come to pass.*

These events included the siege of Jerusalem, the destruction of the Jewish Temple, and the scattering of the Jewish people to the nations. This means that the abomination of desolation had already been fulfilled prior to the book of Revelation. Likewise, the beginning of sorrows (or birth pains) had already begun, and the great tribulation was already well underway by the time the book was written.

Knowing this, John referred to himself as "your brother and companion *in the tribulation*" in his opening remarks of the book of Revelation.

> I, John, both your brother and companion in the tribulation and kingdom and patience of Jesus Christ, was on the island that is called Patmos for the word of God and for the testimony of Jesus Christ.[1]

With the destruction of the Temple behind them, the first-century Church continued to thrive in spite of the tribulation all around them. They had already discerned that the Lord was counting time in terms of prophetic thousand-year Days. Peter's second epistle, written sometime between AD 65 and 68, admonished believers not to overlook "this one thing," that with the Lord one Day is as a thousand years, and a thousand years as one Day.

They understood that the Lord's return was definitely not tardy, for a third-Day return required the completion of two prior Days before its arrival. In this way, believers could monitor the prophetic times (*chronos*) such that all could see the Day approaching.

As they pondered Jesus's Olivet teaching, they also realized that the great tribulation would continue until the sign of His coming appeared. The darkening of the sun, moon, and stars would signal the end of the tribulation of those days and the coming of the Day of the Lord.

Since this "Day" also marked the time of Israel's third-Day revival, the early apostles knew that the Jewish people would not

---

[1]   Revelation 1:9

return to their Land *until that Day drew near*. Today, believers in our time have witnessed the return of the Jewish people to the land of Israel. The seasonal signs (*kairos*) of spring observed in the "fig tree" tell us that summer (the Lord's return) is very near.

So for us, the combination of the prophetic times (*chronos*) and the seasonal signs (*kairos*) converging upon our generation can only mean one thing—*the realization that the end of this age is upon us.*

17

The Revelation from Above

First and foremost, the last book in the Bible is a revelation *of* Jesus Christ in all of His glory. He is the featured attraction throughout the book. He is the One who lives, and was dead, and is alive forevermore. He is the Alpha and Omega, the beginning and the end, the One who is and who was and who is to come, the Almighty!

But the book is also a revelation *from* Him as well. As such, it mirrors His Olivet Discourse by recounting how this present age will end with the sign of His coming, His visible return and the gathering of His elect to heaven.

But the prophecy doesn't end there, for it picks up where His Olivet teaching left off by giving us a series of visions concerning the last half of Daniel's seventieth week. These visions depict the events that will happen during the final years leading up to the battle of Armageddon, including how God's wrath will fall upon the nations in *that Day*.

Since both teachings come from Jesus Himself, whatever we learned about His coming from His Olivet teaching can be applied to the book of Revelation as well. Jesus is not confused about His own return, and He most certainly does not contradict Himself.

Therefore, a proper understanding of the Olivet Discourse enables us to understand the book of Revelation also. Conversely, if we are confused about what He taught from the Mount of Olives, we will probably be confused about the things He revealed from the heavenly Mount Zion as well.

Sadly, the last book in the Bible remains a mystery to most believers. I attribute this to the fact that believers in prior centuries eventually lost sight of God's great Week of thousand-year Days; the truth that Daniel's seventieth week is about the first and second coming of Christ, not the Antichrist; and that Jesus's Olivet Discourse is about the coming of the Son of Man for His Bride, not the final years of the son of perdition.

As a result, our generation inherited a lot of confusion from previous generations. We were told that the thousand years of Christ's reign were not to be taken literally. Those who still did often lost sight of its connection to the Day of the Lord and the seventh Day.

We were told that the Antichrist was the featured attraction of Daniel's seventieth week. Once Christ was booted out of the prophecy, the unfortunate notion of a future seven-year tribulation was born.

We were told that the abomination of desolation, an event so critical to a proper understanding of the Olivet Discourse, no longer defined the siege of Jerusalem as witnessed by first-century believers. Instead, it was relegated to the distant future and redefined as the midpoint of a supposed seven-year tribulation involving the Antichrist.

We were told that the great tribulation no longer defined Hosea's lengthy two Days of being torn and stricken. Instead, it was reduced in length to a mere three and one-half years and redefined as being the latter part of our "seven-year tribulation"—the sacred measure handed down to us for interpreting nearly all end-time prophecies.

We were told that Jesus's Olivet Discourse concerned the Jews who must endure the final years of the Antichrist, that it had virtually nothing to do with the rapture, and that the "real" second coming was reserved for the battle of Armageddon.

By the time we got to the book of Revelation, our minds were so confused that we couldn't help but see the Antichrist represented by the four horsemen of the apocalypse as well. No wonder most pastors and believers shun this last book.

We have given the Antichrist much more attention than what the Scriptures actually allow him. He does not belong in the prophecy of Daniel's seventieth week. Nor does he belong in Jesus's Olivet Discourse. And most certainly, he is not the focus of the first six seals of the book of Revelation.

We know this because the events portrayed in the sixth seal *are an exact match* of what Jesus taught about His coming in the Olivet Discourse. The seal begins with the sign of His coming, announcing the end of the tribulation of those days and the advent of the Day of the Lord.

Once the sun, moon, and stars are darkened, the seal depicts Christ's visible return as the heavens unfold and the inhabitants of the earth mourn.

The seal concludes with the gathering of His elect from the four winds—those who were "counted worthy" to escape the snare of that Day to stand before the Son of Man. As the true Israel of God, this innumerable multitude—gathered out of every tribe, tongue, people, and nation—are shown standing before the throne of God and praising Him for their salvation.

With His Bride having been safely removed to heaven in the rapture, the seventh seal in the book of Revelation depicts God's wrath upon the nations via the seven angelic trumpeters of judgment.

Jesus's prior teaching from "down below," therefore, enables us to understand His revelation from "up above." By comparing both teachings, *we have a definitive marker* in that the sixth seal depicts Christ's return at the end of this present age. It, therefore, divides *this age* from *the age to come.*

Using the prophetic terms associated with God's great Week, the sixth seal marks the end of the sixth great Day and the start of the seventh—the great and awesome Day of the Lord.

Since the sixth seal marks Christ's return at the end of this age, we can only conclude *that the prior five seals all relate to this present age as well*—the period of birth pains, sorrows, tribulation, and persecution with which we are all so familiar.

And since this present age will end with the sixth seal, *the seventh seal must relate to the age to come.* Therefore, the things depicted once this seventh seal has been opened must be "seventh-Day events" that transpire in the age to come.

This includes the wrath of God released by the seven trumpets, the ministry of the two witnesses in Jerusalem, Israel's "third-Day revival" predicted by Hosea, the image set up by the false prophet, the infamous mark of the beast, the final seven bowls of God's wrath, the destruction of the mysterious "Babylon the Great," and finally, the battle of Armageddon itself. These are all events consigned to the age to come. They are not depicted *until after the seventh seal has been removed and John eats the "little book" to prophesy further.*

We can now see why none of these "seventh-Day events" were mentioned by Jesus in His Olivet Discourse. He knew that they would not happen during this present age. Therefore, they did not apply to His Church. The pressing need to reveal the rapture was much more critical in the time that they had left together.

So whatever truths we gained from His Olivet Discourse must hold true in the book of Revelation also. Since Christ's second coming is definitively marked by the opening of the sixth seal, the events that happen afterward in the book of Revelation *can only relate to the last half of Daniel's seventieth week.* This explains why this three-and-one-half-year time frame is repeated several times—in Revelation 11:3, 12:6, 12:14, and 13:5.

The flimsy notion of a future seven-year tribulation, derived solely from a faulty interpretation of Daniel's seventieth week, distorted our entire view of the end times. This was only compounded by the corruption of end-time terms such as *abomination of desolation* and *great tribulation.*

The final die was cast when we lost sight of God's great Week by diminishing the value of prophetic "Days in His sight" to mean mere timelessness. The "last Day" was reduced to mean "someday," and even worse, "any unexpected day."

All we had left to go on were the "signs" of the times. And those who no longer believed in future prophecy tried to diminish those as well by saying they were figuratively fulfilled in the past.

If I didn't know any better, I would almost think that "someone" has been behind a concerted effort to make the Bride lose interest in the return of her own Bridegroom. Perhaps that "someone" doesn't want us to read the end of the Book and find out that we win, and he loses!

It is time for our generation to discard the inferior notions of previous generations and return to the doctrine of the founding apostles. We are called to "rebuild the old ruins" and "repair the desolations of many generations."[1]

As a younger believer, I also used to teach many of the "things we were told." I taught those things for many years. But I refuse to teach them anymore. I am more concerned about His reputation, not mine.

Besides, the light of that soon-approaching Day is suddenly making everything much clearer now. Back then, we did the best we could do with the scant amount of light that was available.

Therefore, I honor and commend all those who kept the truth alive that Jesus was coming back—even when we had to squint to peer through all the shadows. Truly, their reward will be great in that Day.

---

[1] Isaiah 61:4

18

The Scroll of Inheritance

> And I saw in the right hand of Him who sat on
> the throne a scroll written inside and on the back,
> sealed with seven seals. (Rev. 5:1)

The Scroll that was sealed seven times is one of the central features of the book of Revelation. It is the Scroll of Inheritance. This heavenly inheritance has been passed on from God the Father to Jesus Christ, His firstborn Son.

The decree written within the Scroll grants its Recipient the right "to sit at God's right hand," "a name above all names," and "all authority, both in Heaven and in the earth."

The passage in Hebrews 1:1–4 reveals that Jesus *earned these rights* by setting aside His glory to be identified with mankind so that He could purge our sins on the cross. Because of His obedience, God has appointed Jesus to be heir of all things…

> Through whom He also made the worlds; who
> being the brightness of His glory and the express
> image of His person, and upholding all things by
> the word of His power, when He had by Himself

purged our sins, sat down at the right hand of
the Majesty on high, having become so much
better than the angels, as He has by inheritance
obtained a more excellent name than they.

It is important to understand that Jesus is not seated at the
Father's right hand *solely* because He has always been part of the eternal godhead. Instead, it is because He chose to be made a little lower
than the angels for the suffering of death that He might deliver us
from this dreaded enemy.

Because of this, He was crowned with glory and honor and is
seated at God's right hand as the Son of Man.[1] Have you ever wondered why Jesus so often referred to Himself as the Son of Man? It is
because this title fully sums up His mission: He became the Son of
Man *so that we might become the sons of God.*

This inheritance now belongs to Jesus *and to those who are "in
Him,"*—to those who have been "called out" to become the Church
of the Firstborn.

One of the Scroll's provisions appears in the following segment
of the second Psalm:

> I will declare the decree: The Lord has said to
> Me, "You are My Son, Today I have begotten
> You. Ask of Me, and I will give You the nations
> for Your inheritance and the ends of the earth for
> Your possession.
>
> You shall break them with a rod of iron; You shall
> dash them to pieces like a potter's vessel."

Even though the Son already possesses the Scroll, He was told
"to sit and wait" before acting upon this particular provision—until
the proper time for His enemies to be made His footstool. Therefore,
in Psalm 110:1–2, David wrote,

---

[1]   Hebrews 2:5–11

> The Lord said to my Lord, "Sit at My right hand, till I make your enemies Your footstool." The Lord shall send the rod of Your strength out of Zion. Rule in the midst of Your enemies.

The psalmist prophesied that the time would come when the Father would send "the rod of Jesus's strength" out of Zion so that He might rule in the midst of His enemies, so that He might break them with a rod of iron and smash the ungodly nations into broken vessels.

This is what the nation of Israel expected their Messiah to do when Jesus came the first time. Instead, He offered Himself as a sacrificial Lamb, arose from the dead, and ascended to heaven to "sit and wait."

This begs the question, "What is the Father waiting for? When will He make Jesus's enemies His footstool? Quite simply, the Father is waiting for the "other heirs" to be assembled. As joint heirs with Christ, this part of the Scroll cannot be acted upon until "those who overcome" are fully present and accounted for. In Revelation 2:26–27, Jesus made the following promise to His fellow heirs, saying,

> And he who overcomes and keeps My works until the end, to him I will give power over the nations—"He shall rule them with a rod of iron; they shall be dashed to pieces like the potter's vessels"—as I also have received from My Father.

Jesus is waiting for "the body of Christ" to be completed, the "Church of the Firstborn" to be built, His Temple of "Living Stones" to be erected, and "His Bride" to be with Him at the Father's right hand. In His sovereignty, our heavenly Father has allotted two prophetic Days for these things.

> God, who at various times and in various ways spoke in time past to the fathers by the prophets,

has in these last Days spoken to us by His Son,
whom He has appointed heir of all things... [2]

The "various times" associated with "past time" refer to the four prophetic Days that spanned the time from the creation of Adam to the ministry of Christ. The addition of two more Days for building His Church brings us to the end of this age, the return of Christ, and the dawn of the seventh Day. The Bible refers to this seven-Day scheme as *the prophetic times.*

The removal of the seven seals on the Scroll of Inheritance focuses our attention on "these last Days," when God would speak to us through His Son. It reveals that our inheritance will be complete at the seventh Day.

This is the prophetic message emphasized by John's vision of the opening of the scroll. The breaking of each seal yields a vision, a "come and see," in which the things that Jesus told His Church on the Mount of Olives are both repeated and confirmed—only this time, as the One who lives, and was dead, but is alive forevermore.

---

[2]   Hebrews 1:1–2

19

This Age Unsealed

Since the sixth seal depicts Christ's return at the end of this age, the prior five seals provide a review of what Jesus taught about this present age when He was with His disciples on the Mount of Olives. Therefore, these five seals give us a heavenly perspective of the birth pains, tribulation, and persecution that we would see until the end of this age.

As the first four seals are opened (Rev. 6:1–8), each of the four "living beings" that attend God's throne invite us to "come and see" *what they see*. The first living being is like a lion, the second is like a calf, the third has a face like a man, and the fourth is like a flying eagle. Each living being has six wings and is "full of eyes around and within."[1]

This means that they *see everything*! Nothing escapes their attention. They not only see everything that happens *all around*, in both the "seen and unseen realms," *but every inner motive as well.*

> Now I saw when the Lamb opened one of the seals, and I heard one of the four living beings

---

[1]   Revelation 4:7–8

saying with a loud voice like thunder, "Come and see."

And I looked, and behold, a white horse. He who sat on it had a bow; and a crown was given to him, and he went out conquering and to conquer.

These spiritual horsemen are, as Paul described them, "the rulers of the darkness of this age" and "the wicked spirits in the heavens."[2] Since the fourth rider is a spirit of death, working in tandem with Hades, it follows that the other horsemen are wicked spirits as well.

Therefore, the white-horse rider is a ruling spirit of darkness promoting false religions, false christs, and false prophets. He is a deceiving angel of light, charged by Satan to sow deception throughout the earth. This spirit stands in sharp contrast to Jesus, who also appears on a white horse later in Revelation 19:11:

And behold, a white horse; and He who sat on Him was called Faithful and True.

In His Olivet teaching, Jesus said, "Take heed that no one deceives you. For many will come in My name, saying, 'I am the Christ,' and will deceive many."

Notice that Jesus said "many will come." Since this deceiving spirit has been blinding men and women throughout the course of this present age, it is incorrect to teach that this seal merely depicts the Antichrist.

Bear in mind that we are not viewing a future seven-year tribulation. Instead, the vision relates to what Jesus said about the beginning of sorrows, saying, "And you will hear of wars and rumors of wars. See that you are not troubled, *for all these things must come to pass, but the end is not yet.* For nation will rise against nation, and kingdom against kingdom." Likewise, the second seal reveals,

---

2   Ephesians 6:12

> When He opened the second seal, I heard the second living being saying, "Come and see."

> Another horse, fiery red, went out. And it was granted to the one who sat on it to take peace from the earth, and that people should kill one another; and there was given to him a great sword.

The red-horse rider is a spirit promoting warfare and racial violence. This spirit sows hatred among humanity such that nations and ethnic groups clash with one another. He promotes racial injustice such that men hate one another simply because the color of their skin is a few shades darker or lighter. His grant of power comes from Satan, not God. God does, however, monitor their actions and set limits on what they can do.

The combination of the first two seals also reveals another critical feature of this present age: the combination of a false religion bent on conquering the world with a "great sword" has sponsored many of the wars that have occurred over the past two millennia. The terror of this false religion is still felt around the world today.

> When He opened the third seal, I heard the third living being say, "Come and see."

> I looked, and behold, a black horse, and he who sat on it had a pair of scales in his hand. And I heard a voice in the midst of the four living beings saying, "A quart of wheat for a denarius (a full day's pay), and three quarts of barley for a denarius; and do not harm the oil and the wine."

Nearly two thousand years ago, Jesus continued His discourse on the coming sorrows, saying, "And there will be famines…"

The spirit who rides the black horse is a spirit of poverty. He is charged with bringing lack and economic ruin upon the earth, whether by famine, drought, hyperinflation, currency devaluation, greed, stock market crashes, and so forth.

Poverty always follows religious deception; and warfare always creates refugees, economic ruin, and the lack of essential human needs among the populations who suffer in the line of fire. These things are not coming someday, for they have characterized the entire course of this age. The persistence of third-world famines in our lifetimes is a case in point.

Jesus concluded his discussion on the beginning of birth pains by saying, "And there will be pestilences and earthquakes in various places. All these are the beginning of birth pains." Similarly, the fourth seal reveals,

> When he opened the fourth seal, I heard the voice of the fourth living being saying, "Come and see."

> I looked, and behold, a pale horse. And the name of him who sat on it was Death, and Hades followed with him. And power was given to them over a fourth of the earth, to kill with sword, with hunger, with death, and by the beasts of the earth.

This spirit promotes all forms of death and destruction, whether by sickness, disease, pestilence, violence, or natural calamity.

These birth pains began shortly after Jesus's time and have continued to gain momentum such that our generation now stands on the brink of global disaster from every front. The good news for believers is that the increasing severity of these birthing pains can only signal one thing, *the realization that the birth of the sons of God is very near.*

Like the apostle Paul, we can say, "For I consider that the sufferings of this present time are not worthy to be compared with the glory which shall be revealed in us, for the earnest expectation of the creation eagerly waits for the revealing of the sons of God."[3]

So keep your eyes on the *prize*, and trust Him to keep you "in all of your ways." Know also that "to be absent from the body is to be present with the Lord." For us as believers, physical death is nothing more than stepping into the realm of His eternal glory.

Jesus concluded this segment of His Olivet teaching by saying, "Then they will deliver you up to tribulation and kill you, and you will be hated by all nations for My Name's sake." Since the seals parallel His teaching, the fifth seal reveals,

> When He opened the fifth seal, I saw under the altar the souls of those who had been slain for the word of God and for the testimony which they held.
>
> And they cried with a loud voice, saying, "How long, O Lord, holy and true, until You judge and avenge our blood on those who dwell on the earth?" Then a white robe was given to them that they should rest a little while longer, until both the number of their fellow servants and their brethren, who would be killed as they, was completed.

So far, the first five seals have reiterated the things that Jesus taught His disciples in that they would see persecution, sorrowful birth pains, and great tribulation until the end of this age. In John's Gospel, Jesus said, "In the world you will have tribulation; but be of good cheer, for I have overcome the world."[4]

We need not fear the great tribulation. You have lived your entire life in the midst of it. The good news is that the dawning of

---

[3]   Romans 8:18

[4]   John 16:33

the third Day is nearly upon us. Soon, "the tribulation of those days" will be over.

It is also helpful to understand that the release of these seals *do not initiate these events on the earth. Nor do they cause these things to happen.* This is because the sorrows portrayed by these seals do not represent the wrath of God. He is not the One afflicting the world with these sorrows. Instead, they are the actions of the god of this world—the Thief who comes to steal, kill, and destroy. *This part of the vision was granted so that we would understand who is behind these sorrows.*

Therefore, as we move on to the sixth seal, keep in mind that these seals are tracking the same scenario of events that Jesus previously discussed in His Discourse. So in essence, these first five seals have depicted what has been nearly two thousand years of great tribulation, or as Jesus called it—the tribulation of those Days.

20

Rending the Heavens

In His Olivet Discourse, Jesus said, "Immediately after the tribulation of those days the sun will be darkened, and the moon will not give its light; the stars will fall from heaven, and the powers of the heavens will be shaken."

"Then the sign of the Son of Man will appear in heaven, and then all the tribes of the earth will mourn, and they will see the Son of Man coming on the clouds of heaven with power and great glory."

Since the seals are following the same scenario that Jesus laid out in His Olivet teaching, we would expect to see something very similar to the passage above as the sixth seal is opened.

> I looked when He opened the sixth seal, and behold, there was a great earthquake; and the sun became black as sackcloth of hair, and the moon became like blood. And the stars of heaven fell to the earth as a fig tree drops its late figs when it is shaken by a mighty wind.

While "blood-moon omens" can tell us that we're getting closer, the celestial sign of darkness in the sun, moon, and stars will notify watchful believers that it is time to "look up and lift up our heads."

Jesus said that the stars will fall from heaven. Likewise, the sixth seal depicts the stars of heaven falling to the earth as figs shaken from a fig tree in a violent storm.

It is obvious that these "falling stars" do not refer to the heavenly bodies that form the constellations high above us. Our own sun is rather small compared to the other stars in our galaxy. A collision with our own sun alone would obliterate our entire planet.

So what did Jesus mean by falling stars? Will the earth have a close encounter with a comet and pass through its tail? Could it be that the earth will be bombarded by a shower of meteors, or by an approaching asteroid as it breaks apart in our atmosphere?

And what did Jesus mean when He told us to look up and expect His return "when we see these things *begin to happen?*" Both Matthew's account and the account in the sixth seal make it sound like these things happen quite suddenly and all at once. So how can it be said that they "begin to happen"?

Once again, Luke's account sheds some important light on what Jesus meant. Luke revealed that the nations of the earth will be distressed, in anguish, and perplexed when the signs in the sun, moon, and stars appear.

The next verse says, "Men fainting for fear and for expectation of the things coming upon the inhabited earth, for the powers of the heavens will be shaken."[1]

The things which are coming on the earth obviously relate to the shaking of the "powers of the heavens." The *Amplified Bible* adds, "For the [very] powers of the heavens will be shaken and caused to totter." NIV says, "Men will faint from terror, apprehensive of what is coming on the world, for the heavenly bodies will be shaken."

Luke's insightful remarks reveal that mankind *will know in advance that "these things" are coming!* This explains why the nations

---

[1]   Luke 21:25–26 (A. S. Worrell's Translation)

will be perplexed, distressed, and fainting with fear. It is because of "the expectation" that these things are coming upon the earth.

Our technology now allows us to track the orbits of "the heavenly bodies" that travel throughout our solar system, including comets and asteroids. There is a problem, however, in that we have not yet discovered all of the objects that could potentially collide with our planet. Even if our instruments were to detect an asteroid headed our way, there is really very little we can do about it.

It would appear then from Luke's account that this fearful scenario is exactly what will happen. The nations will be full of fear due to the "expectation of those things which are coming on the earth." Even though they will know that they are coming, they will be perplexed as to how to prevent the approaching calamities.

Believers, on the other hand, will know why these things are coming. We will know that the time has come for God to shake not only the earth but the heavens also.

Apparently, the first effects of this "shaking" will cause the sun, moon, and stars to grow dark as viewed from the vantage point of our atmosphere. Joel prophesied, "The sun and moon will grow dark, and the stars will diminish their brightness."[2]

The prophet Isaiah made a similar prediction: "Behold, the Day of the Lord comes… for the stars of heaven and their constellations will not give their light; the sun will be darkened in its going forth, and the moon will not cause its light to shine."[3]

Notice that nothing is said in either of these prophecies about the stars falling from heaven. This means that the diminishment of sunlight, moonlight, and starlight all across the planet will be seen *before these coming calamities actually occur.*

To clarify, the appearance of celestial darkness is the precursory sign of His coming. The stars falling to earth relate to the actual wrath of that Day. *The rapture will occur in between these two celestial events.*

---

[2]   Joel 3:15

[3]   Isaiah 13:9–10

This explains how believers will be able to see these things *begin to happen* and, thereby, know that the Day of our redemption is nearly upon us. As the rest of the world fears the approaching gloom, we will rejoice knowing that we are about to see the approaching Groom.

While I cannot say how much advanced warning the world will have before these calamities strike the earth, watchful believers will no doubt use this opportunity to bring as many to Christ as possible.

I do, however, know this much: the Lord will rend the heavens and catch us away just in the nick of time. We will, therefore, be saved from the snare of that Day and "escape *all these things* that will come to pass."

Sitting, Then Coming

The revelation of the sixth seal continues,

> Then the sky receded as a scroll when it is rolled up, and every mountain and island was moved out of its place.

Even though it is not directly stated in the sixth seal, Jesus's Olivet teaching assures us that He will suddenly appear at this moment, for in the midst of all the fear and darkness, as the sky folds up like a scroll, and as the veil is rent to expose the unseen realm of His glory, *our light will come!* The glory of the Lord will arise upon us, and we will all shine.

In Matthew's Olivet account, Jesus revealed that the celestial signs would be followed by *the sign of the Son of Man appearing in heaven*. There is a subtle distinction between His "appearing in heaven" and His "visible descent in the clouds with power and great glory."

The reason for this distinction is important. The Jewish leaders arrested and tried Jesus *in secret*. But His heavenly Father will declare His vindication *openly*.

At His trial, the Lamb spoke like a King, saying, "Hereafter, you will see *the Son of Man sitting* at the right hand of the Mighty One, *and coming* on the clouds of heaven." Note the order—first sitting, then coming.

The Father wants the world to know that this same Jesus, crucified by both Jews and Gentiles alike, is not only alive but has been given a name above every other name. So at His appearing, the Father will officially present Him to the world as being both Lord and Christ.

Though He was despised and rejected of men, the Father accepted Him as the rightful Heir to sit at His right hand of Power. Therefore, the world will be given a solemn moment of reflection to behold the awesome majesty of Jesus Christ—the Son of the living God and the risen Son of Man. He will be gloriously unveiled in His seated position of honor and glory for all to see.

Once He appears, everyone will witness the Lord's descent in the clouds of heaven with power and great glory. Then all the tribes (or peoples) of the earth will mourn.[4] Revelation 1:7 states, "Behold, He is coming with the clouds, and every eye will see Him, even those who pierced Him. And all the tribes of the earth will mourn because of Him." Isaiah 40:5 adds, "The glory of the Lord shall be revealed and all flesh will see it together."

The sixth seal attests to these things by revealing,

> And the kings of the earth, the great men, the rich men, the commanders, the mighty men, every slave and every free man, hid themselves in the caves and in the rocks of the mountains, and said to the mountains and rocks, "Fall on us and hide us from the face of Him who sits on the throne and from the wrath of the Lamb!
>
> For the great Day of His wrath has come, and who is able to stand?"

---

4   Matthew 24:30

21

The Look from Afar

The sixth seal confirms the truth that Christ's coming in the rapture will not be a secret event. Instead, every eye will see Him when He comes. This does not mean, however, that everyone will participate in the rapture. It is one thing to see Him. It is quite another thing to be looking for Him.

The appearance of the throne of God will cause those who are ashamed to run and hide, just as Adam and Eve hid when the Lord came looking for them. They will cry out, "Hide us from the face of Him who sits on the throne and from the wrath of the Lamb."

Because of this, the apostle John admonished his little children to "abide in Him, that when He appears, we may have confidence *and not be ashamed before Him at His coming.*"[1] It is important to have confidence when He appears. He wants us to come boldly to the throne of His grace.

To that end, the Spirit has been preparing His Bride for that Day with messages of His abundant grace. He is affirming us in the love of the Father so that all fear and dread of His presence can be

---

[1]   1 John 2:28

cast out. If you wait until the last minute to gain this confidence, you might miss out.

The apostle John wrote, "Love has been perfected among us in this: that *we may have boldness in the Day of Judgment*, because as He is, so are we in this world."[2] Now is the time to make peace with God by believing on His Son. If you are bold now, you will have no problem being bold when that Day arrives.

With the heavens opened and His Son properly introduced, the holy entourage will begin. The participants in this heavenly parade will consist of archangels, angelic charioteers, and the departed saints in Christ, all led by the Lord Himself. It will be glorious.

The prophet Ezekiel witnessed a preview of this coming attraction and recorded the vision in the first chapter of his book. It is worth taking the time to read, for it reveals how the Lord will be "admired among all who believe when He comes in that Day."[3]

The Shadow Cast by His Crucifixion

Someone might ask, "But if everyone sees the Lord when He comes in that Day, how is it that people will miss out on the rapture?" The answer can be found in the prophetic shadow cast by Christ's crucifixion.

The similarity of the crucifixion account in Matthew 27:45–55 with the events portrayed in the sixth seal are too uncanny to be a coincidence. The sixth seal begins with a great earthquake in conjunction with the darkening of the sun, moon, and stars.

Similarly, Matthew's account of the crucifixion states, "Now from the sixth hour until the ninth hour *there was darkness over the land.*" Verse 51 also tells us that *the earth quaked* and that *the rocks were split.*

At this point, the veil of the temple was torn in two from top to bottom. The rending of the veil, separating the Holy of Holies from

---

[2]   1 John 4:17

[3]   2 Thessalonians 1:10

the rest of the temple, *exposed that which had previously been hidden for all to see.*

Likewise, the veil that separates this natural realm from the realm of the unseen will be "torn in two from top to bottom" as that Day begins. Every eye will see the heavenly Holy of Holies.

The next verse in Matthew states, "And the *graves were opened*; and many bodies of the saints who had fallen asleep were raised; and coming out of the graves, *appeared to many.*" In like fashion, the sixth seal portrays Christ's return in which the dead in Christ will come up out of their graves and appear.

The parallel between the two accounts was an intentional act of God. The opening of the graves during the crucifixion was a preview of what to expect once the celestial signs of the sixth seal appear.

This cancels out the concept of a secret coming. It will in fact be just the opposite. Every eye will see Him. It will be a veil-rending event that captures the attention of everyone on the planet. It will be like lightning—you cannot help but see it.

The Gospel of Matthew states that when the soldiers who were guarding the cross "*saw the earthquake and the things that had happened, they feared greatly,* saying, "Truly this was the Son of God." Similarly, the sixth seal reveals that men will hide themselves "in the caves and in the rocks of the mountains for fear."

When the Lord returns, the sight of the heavenly realm unfolding before men's eyes and the resplendent glory of God will be overwhelming. The natural instinct of the flesh when encountering such glory is to run and hide or faint in fear. Don't let your own heart deceive you on this matter. If you never invited Christ into your heart by the time that He appears, you will instinctively turn away in shame at the presence of His glory.

On the other hand, if you turn to Him now and eagerly look for His return, just as a bride eagerly anticipates the day of her wedding, His love will cast out all fear, and His Spirit will rise up within you at that moment with a holy boldness.

This truth is foreshadowed as the account of the crucifixion continues in verse 55:

> And many women who followed Jesus from Galilee, ministering to Him, were there looking from afar, among whom were Mary Magdalene, Mary the mother of James and Joseph, and the mother of Zebedee's sons.

It is noteworthy that the passage only mentions women. I believe that the Holy Spirit recorded it this way so that we might view these women as a type of the Bride of Christ.

The passage also says that they were "looking from afar." This is significant. Just as the women were looking from a distance in terms of geography, Christ's Bride is looking from a distance *in terms of time*.

True biblical faith sees from a distance what others can only see after the fact. The world says, "I'll believe it when I see it." In contrast, those of faith have a pleasing habit of saying, "I'll see it *because* I believe it."

Therefore, just like these faithful women, the Bride of Christ has been "looking from afar" for His return. Fixing our gaze from such a distance guarantees that we will have boldness in that Day.

As discussed previously, the passage in Isaiah 40:29–31 assures us that those who wait on the Lord will mount up with wings as eagles. The shadow formed around Christ's crucifixion projects this same truth, for it tells us that "the women followed Jesus from Galilee, *ministering to Him*." To "wait on the Lord" simply means to be in a posture of *faith and expectation*. This is what ministers to the Lord. It is a faith thing, not a works thing. Such boldhearted ones will escape the snare of that Day to stand before the Son of Man in heaven.

Those who miss the gathering (rapture), however, will still have an opportunity to confess along with the Centurion, "Surely, this was the Son of God." I believe that many from around the world will ultimately receive Christ after He has appeared. The Bible reveals that the remnant of the nation of Israel will turn to Him at that time, confessing, "Blessed is He who comes in the name of the Lord."

Others will no doubt dismiss what they have seen and reinterpret the event after their initial panic subsides. This is where the deception of the Antichrist comes in. He will no doubt "spin the event" and cause some people to believe a lie.

Could this explain the recent popularity of the chariots of the gods, ancient aliens, and the UFO phenomenon? Will this be part of the deception promoted by the Antichrist? Will he attempt to rally the world over the thought that we need to defend our planet from an alien invasion?

The idea that the rapture could happen at any *unexpected* moment has greatly distorted our understanding of the Lord's return. Because of this, the rapture is often ridiculed as being a destructive event in which the disappearance of believers will cause the death of thousands of people as cars collide and planes drop from the sky.

It is my personal conviction that the Holy Spirit will stir our hearts when it is time to look up. Since that Day will not come upon watchful believers unexpectedly, our hearts will be occupied with great anticipation, not our daily routines.

It is time to return to a New Testament view of His coming in that Day. Soon, the realm of the unseen will become fully visible. It is important for those who wish to escape and stand *to see it now—from afar*. The passage in Hebrews 9:28 states,

> So Christ was offered once to bear the sins of many. To those who eagerly wait for Him He will appear a second time, apart from sin, for salvation.

The question is not whether He will appear to you. The question is whether He will appear *for salvation*.

22

Gathered from the Four Winds

In His Olivet Discourse, Jesus taught, "Then the sign of the Son of Man will appear in Heaven, and then all the tribes of the earth will mourn, and they will see the Son of Man coming on the clouds of Heaven with power and great glory."

The sixth seal maintains this same sequence of events, for it opened with the celestial signs, followed by the rending of the heavens to reveal God's throne and then Christ's visible descent. The sixth chapter concluded with the inhabitants of the earth mourning and crying out, "For the great Day of His wrath has come, and who is able to stand?"

As we will see, the seventh and last seal on the scroll depicts God's wrath in the Day of the Lord. Since this seal is not opened until chapter 8, *chapter 7 depicts what will happen as Jesus descends, but before His wrath strikes the earth.*

So when we refer back to Jesus's Olivet teaching, the next thing He said was,

> And He will send His angels with a great sound of a trumpet, and they will gather together His elect from the four winds, from one end of heaven to the other.

This means that chapter 7 is all about "the gathering His elect." Just as He promised, we will be gathered by His angels before the wrath of the Day of the Lord comes. *Therefore, John's vision devotes an entire chapter to the rapture.*

It is interesting that the rapture appears in chapter 7, just as the seventh great Day begins and as the sixth seal of this age concludes.

In His earthly teaching, Jesus said that He would gather us "from the four winds." At first, we might think that this expression merely refers to the four points of the compass, meaning He will gather us from the north, south, east, and west. And while it is certainly true that His angels will gather us from all around the world, chapter 7 begins by revealing *what Jesus really meant by being gathered from the four winds.*

The Four Angels and the Four Winds

The chapter opens by revealing that these "four winds" will harm the earth and bring destruction to our planet. Later in chapter 8, we will see that these winds correspond to God *shaking the powers of the heavens.*

The chapter also reveals that four angels are in charge of this wrath, "to whom it was granted to harm the earth and the sea." Yet they are also told to restrain this wrath and wait for the appropriate time to release these winds upon the earth. The passage begins,

> After these things I saw four angels standing at the four corners of the earth, holding [back] the four winds of the earth, that the wind should not blow on the earth, on the sea, or on any tree.

> Then I saw another angel ascending from the east, having the seal of the living God. And he cried with a loud voice to the four angels, to whom it was granted to harm the earth and the sea, saying,

"Do not harm the earth, the sea, or the trees till we have sealed the servants of God on their foreheads."

The truth that these four angels are connected to God shaking the powers of the heavens is indisputable. They reappear in chapter 8, just as the seventh seal is removed from the scroll and the wrath of that Day begins.

The first angel appears in verse 7. "The first angel sounded: And hail and fire followed, mingled with blood, and they were thrown to the earth. And a third of the trees were burned up, and all green grass was burned up."

The second angel of the four winds appears in the next verse. "Then the second angel sounded: And something like a great mountain burning with fire was thrown into the sea, and a third of the sea became blood. And a third of the living creatures in the sea died, and a third of the ships were destroyed."

The third angel is featured in verse 10. "Then the third angel sounded: And a great star fell from heaven, burning like a torch, and it fell on a third of the rivers and on the springs of water. The name of the star is Wormwood…and many men died from the water because it was made bitter."

Finally, the fourth angelic wind is depicted in verse 12. "Then the fourth angel sounded: And a third of the sun was struck, a third of the moon, and a third of the stars, so that a third of them were darkened. A third of the day did not shine, and likewise the night."

As you can see, these four winds have been decreed by God to harm the earth, the sea, and the trees. The trees and grass will be burned up. The sea and the waves will roar as great tsunamis deluge coastal cities. Ships will be destroyed, and the waters will be poisoned.

This destruction will come upon the earth from above as God shakes the powers of the heavens. This heavenly shaking will result in objects falling from the sky, such as fiery hail, a burning mountain (asteroid), and a star burning like a torch. Isaiah prophesied the following dire warning:

> Fear and the pit and the snare are upon you, O
> inhabitant of the earth. And it shall be that he
> who flees from the noise of the fear shall fall into
> the pit, and he who comes up from the midst of
> the pit shall be caught in the snare;

> For the windows from on high are open, and the
> foundations of the earth are shaken. The earth is
> violently broken; the earth is split open; the earth
> is shaken exceedingly. The earth shall reel to and
> from like a drunkard and totter like a hut.[1]

The calamity caused by the fourth wind will somehow affect either the rotational spin of the earth, the tilt of the earth, or our orbital path around the sun. In Isaiah 13:13, the prophet prophesied again, saying,

> Therefore I will shake the heavens and the earth
> will move out of her place, in the wrath of the
> Lord of hosts and in the Day of His fierce anger.

As I said, even though our technology can detect in advance that a comet or an asteroid is headed our way, the earth stands defenseless against such a heavenly barrage. Jesus said that the expectation of these things coming upon the earth will engender great fear and distress among the nations.

As watchful believers, we need not fear these things for even one moment, for Jesus promised to "cut short" the days of His elect. He promised that His angels will catch us up in chariots of fire into the safety of His Presence. He said that He would enable us to escape the snare of that Day and that we would stand before the Son of Man.

When that Day comes, the nations will lament, saying, "The great Day of His wrath has come, who is able to stand?" In response, *those who know they are His* from all around the world will boldly

---

[1]   Isaiah 24:17–20

proclaim, "We will, for His angels will be sent forth to gather us *from* these harmful winds!"

Since believers can be found in virtually every part of the world, it goes without saying that we will be gathered from every possible direction. Jesus didn't need to tell us that.

Instead, what He wanted us to know was that He would gather us *from* or *out of* the impending danger posed by these four winds *before they begin to blow.* He called John up into heaven from the island of Patmos for this very reason. He gave him this vision to assure our hearts that we will be saved from the wrath to come. Those who "watch" by staying attentive to His written Word will know to "look up" when we see these things begin to happen. We will know that our redemption is drawing near.

We lose all of these revelations and assurances when we misinterpret passages such as the Olivet Discourse and the seven seals of the book of Revelation to be all about the coming of the Antichrist. *Jesus meant them to be about the coming of the Son of Man.*

Eventually, many in the body of Christ will realize that there will be no secret, signless, any-moment coming. Instead, Jesus will come just as He said He would, in clouds of glory for all to see. This realization does not rob us of any faithful provision previously held by a pretribulation or midtribulation rapture. We will not be exposed to the mark of the beast. Nor will we remain to face the image of the beast, the final years of the Antichrist, or the wrath of that Day.

We do not need to debate whether we will miss "the tribulation," because we have already lived our entire lives in the midst of it. Besides, the great tribulation is nearly over.

Soon, the seals that guarantee "our purchased possession" will be removed to stand before the Son of Man and God's glorious throne in heaven. When that Day comes, our Father will write His name on our foreheads as well as the name of His city.[2]

---

[2]   Revelation 14:1 and Revelation 3:12

23

Sealed for the Day of Redemption

And I heard the number of those who were
sealed—144 thousands of all the tribes of Israel.

The seventh chapter opened with a vision of the four angels firmly
holding back the four winds that will shake both heaven and earth in
that Day. They are told to restrain these four winds *until the servants
of God have been sealed on their foreheads.*

Numbering Those without Number

Who are these servants of God, and why do they appear in a
chapter wholly dedicated to the rapture? Interestingly, this mystery
group only appears in one other place in the Bible—in the fourteenth chapter of the book of Revelation to be exact.

Chapter 14 is one of the "minivisions" that further explain the
last half of Daniel's seventieth week. The chapter shows this group
standing together with Jesus before God's throne and singing a new
song *that only they can learn.*

Not only that, the context of the previous chapter shows them in heaven just as the final three and a half years of the Antichrist begin. The purpose of this minivision is to affirm that these "servants of God" are already in heaven *before mankind is warned not to take the mark of the beast.*

As to their identity, we are told that they are undefiled, without deceit, and without fault before the throne of God. We are also told that they were redeemed from among men, that they are "firstfruits" to both God and the Lamb, *and that they follow the Lamb wherever He goes.* It is noteworthy that after Paul described the rapture, he wrote, "And thus we shall always be with the Lord."[1]

Their virginity is another important aspect of their spiritual identity. Therefore, Paul wrote to the Church at Corinth, "For I am jealous for you with godly jealousy; for I have betrothed you to one husband *that I may present you as a chaste virgin to Christ.*"[2] Unlike those who are of this world, they sought none of the other "gods and goddesses" that the world has worshipped.

As to their number, the Greek text uses the word *chiliades,* meaning "thousands," instead of *chilioi,* the singular for thousand. The plural form is used in every instance, including twelve thousands (*chiliades*) from each of the twelve tribes.

So if the *144 thousands* (*chiliades*) were meant to mean a specific number, the Spirit would have used the same Greek word used when Jesus fed the five thousand (*chilioi*).

The fact that there are 144 *thousands* (an indefinite number), and not *144,000* (a definite number), symbolizes an innumerable multitude. So even though this multitude is without number, *they do have a number.*

Twelve is the number of God's people (twelve tribes). It is also the number associated with delegated authority (twelve apostles). When multiplied, we get 144, symbolizing those from among God's people who will have authority to reign with Christ in that Day.

---

[1]   1 Thessalonians 4:17

[2]   2 Corinthians 11:1–2

Therefore, *the 144 thousands* is the official numerical designation of the Bride of Christ. This symbolic number was not meant to confuse us, but to enlighten us. It speaks to the *mystery of Christ*, where there is neither Jew nor Gentile, male or female, bond or free, but a new creation *in Christ*.

The apostle Paul affirmed this new covenant truth when he wrote, "For they are not all Israel who are of Israel." The *Amplified Bible* reads, "For it is not everybody who is a descendant of Jacob [Israel] who belongs to [the true] Israel."

The flip side is also true. There are those who are not the physical descendants of Jacob who belong to the true Israel of God. In the light of new covenant realities, the true "Israel of God" consists of those who have believed on the Lord Jesus Christ.

In other words, the Israel of God is a "faith thing," not a "natural thing." It has nothing to do with biological descent. Instead, it has everything to do with faith in the Lord Jesus Christ.

This does not diminish the promises made to the natural descendants of Abraham. The nation of Israel will stand at the head of the natural nations in that Day. But by then, they will have believed on the Lord Jesus Christ just as His Bride did *prior to that Day.*

Removing the Seal

With this in mind, we can now understand why the symbolic reference of *the 144 thousands* appears in a chapter devoted entirely to the rapture. It is because the 144 thousands *are Christ's elect.* The chapter affirms how His elect will be gathered to heaven before the four winds harm the earth. It also reveals how "our being sealed" will result in the fullness of our salvation in the Day of the Lord.

In Ephesians 4:30, Paul wrote, "And do not grieve the Holy Spirit of God, by whom you were sealed *for the Day of redemption.*" Earlier in his letter, Paul explained the purpose of being sealed.

> In Him you also trusted, after you heard the word of truth, the gospel of your salvation; in

> whom also, having believed, you were sealed with
> the Holy Spirit of promise, who is the guarantee
> of our inheritance until the redemption of the
> purchased possession, to the praise of His glory.[3]

Whenever we believe on the Lord, we are sealed with the Holy Spirit of promise. He is our guarantee that we will receive a glorified body just like Christ's when He returns.

This "sealing process" has been going on now for nearly two Days (or two thousand years). It will continue during the last moments of darkness until the heavens are suddenly rent and the Son of Man appears. Since the four angels are restraining these harmful winds during the time of this sealing, we need only ask, "For how long have they been restraining?"

Once again, we can look to the apostles. Peter wrote, "But the heavens and the earth which *are now preserved* by the same word, *are reserved* for fire *until the Day of Judgment and perdition of ungodly men*."[4]

This means that the heavens and the earth are presently being preserved by God's word. In fact, they were being preserved as early as Peter's time. Jesus promised that these winds will not be allowed to harm the earth until this sealing process has been finished—not until His Church has been built, His Body made complete, and His Bride has been received.

Once that Day comes, the seal (or escrow deposit) guaranteeing our full redemption will be released, just as an escrow deposit is released at a real estate closing.

Right now, we have a promise of future glory. The seal of the Holy Spirit guarantees this glorious promise. The "deal" will be closed and finalized when Jesus returns. At that time, we will receive "the purchased possession"—an immortal body like unto His glorious body.

---

[3]   Ephesians 1:13–14

[4]   2 Peter 3:7

The release of the seal does not mean that His Spirit will leave us. It simply means that *He no longer needs to guarantee that which we have finally obtained.* This is the truth expressed in chapter 7. It depicts the release of the seal in the Day of Redemption.

The strategic symbolism of portraying Christ's Bride via *the 144 thousands* reinforces His promise that He will come again "and receive us to Himself, to His Father's House of many mansions."

As the Bridegroom, Jesus promised that He would go and prepare a place for us. The following passage in Revelation 21:9–17 reveals that this "prepared place" is based on multiples of the number 12. Not only that, its wall just so happens to measure 144 cubits.

> Then one of the seven angels…came to me, saying, "Come, I will show you the bride, the Lamb's wife." And he carried me away in the Spirit to a great and high mountain, and showed me the great city, the holy Jerusalem, descending out of heaven from God, having the glory of God…
>
> And she had a great and high wall with twelve gates, and twelve angels at the gates, and names written on them, which are the twelve tribes of the children of Israel…
>
> Now the wall of the city had twelve foundations, and on them were the names of the twelve apostles of the Lamb… and he measured the city with the reed—twelve thousand furlongs… then he measured its wall—one hundred and forty-four cubits.

It was the angel's mission to show John "the Bride, the Lamb's Wife." *It is significant that John saw this City instead.* The meaning is clear. We are meant to understand that this is our future home. It is our Father's house. Since this is where the Son of Man lives and reigns, it is where the Son's Bride will live and reign also. Forever, she will be at His side.

It is the prepared place of the Lamb's wife—the multiplied thousands of the 144!

24

Standing before the Throne

As we have seen, the numerical value of 144 symbolizes delegated authority, not just the promise of redemption. Accordingly, there are promises made to the "overcoming Church" that do not apply to those who will be saved after the rapture.

For one thing, those who overcome are promised to be given "power over the nations"[1] and to "sit with the Lamb in his throne, just as He overcame [death] and sat down with His Father in His throne."[2]

The promise that we will follow the Lamb wherever He goes also means that we will be caught up to His Father's house *before the shaking of the four winds begins.* Since the trumpet blasts of the four angels do not sound until chapter 8, the vision of the rapture continues in the seventh chapter by revealing,

> After these things I looked, and behold, a great
> multitude which no one could number, of all
> nations, tribes, peoples, and tongues, standing

---

[1]   Revelation 2:26

[2]   Revelation 3:21

before the throne and before the Lamb, clothed
with white robes, with palm branches in their
hands, and crying out with a loud voice, saying,
"Salvation belongs to our God who sits on the
throne, and to the Lamb!"[3]

One of the most obvious features of this multitude is that they
are *standing before the throne and before the Lamb*. This prophetic
phrase marks this multitude as those who "watched and prayed" in
order to escape the coming snare and "to stand before the Son of
Man."

That Day did not come on them unexpectedly. Having "looked
from afar," they knew that it was time to "look up" when they saw
"these things begin to happen." Consequently, they received Christ's
promise to "escape and stand."

The fact that this great multitude is in heaven cannot be denied,
for they are not only standing before the Son of Man *but before God's
throne as well*. They stand in sharp contrast to the martyrs of the fifth
seal who were shown under the altar crying out for vengeance.

Instead, this innumerable multitude is shown celebrating the
"salvation of their God" with loud shouts of praise and the waving of
palm branches before Jesus, their King.

Those who were previously under the altar are now before the
throne along with their fellow brethren who were not martyred as
they were. They are no longer crying out "how long until you avenge
our blood," for they know that the Day of vengeance has come.

At this point, the Lord's Church has been built, and His Body
has been fully gathered to stand together with Him in glory. His
Bride has been fully consummated in that "the two have become one
flesh" through the power of resurrection.

For we are members of His body, of His flesh and
of His bones, "for this reason a man shall leave

---

[3]   Revelation 7:4 and 9–10

his father and mother and be joined to his wife,
and the two shall become one flesh."

This is a great mystery, but I speak concerning
Christ and the Church.[4]

This cancels out the teaching that the Church will be "caught up" at the end of a seven-year tribulation only to meet the Lord coming down at the battle of Armageddon. Such a notion is simply not scriptural.

As joint heirs with Christ, His body must be caught up to stand with Him in heaven *before the seven trumpets of God's wrath can sound.* We will appear before the Throne in order to hear the declaration of the Scroll and to receive "power over the nations." As it turns out, the Church will not be caught up *merely to escape the wrath of that Day but to help administer it along with Him.*

In His Olivet lesson, Jesus gave us the following sequence of events: first, the signs of darkness in the sun, moon, and stars signaling the end of the tribulation of those Days and the advent of the Day of the Lord; next, the visible coming of the Son of Man in the clouds of heaven with power and great glory; then the gathering of His elect from the four winds by His holy angels.

The revelation provided by the sixth seal has confirmed this same scenario; for it began with the signs in the sun, moon, and stars, and concludes with the victorious arrival of Christ's Bride in heaven.

Therefore, the scene before us, wherein we see this great multitude that only God could number, gives us a glimpse of the elect *after they have been gathered in the rapture.*

So that we would be sure to recognize this innumerable multitude as "those who escaped to stand in that Day," an elder approached John and posed the following question to him:

---

4   Ephesians 5:30–32

> Then one of the elders answered, saying to me, "Who are these arrayed in white robes, and where did they come from?" And I said, "Sir, you know."

> So he said to me, "These are the ones who come out of the great tribulation, and washed their robes and made them white in the blood of the Lamb."

The wisdom provided by the elder confirms the length of the great tribulation in that it would extend from the first century of the Church throughout the remainder of this present age just as Jesus taught.

It confirms that those who have believed throughout the two Days of Church building, who were sealed with the Holy Spirit for the Day of Redemption, and who cashed in their seals for the purchased possession all came out of "the great tribulation."

John was in it back in his time, and we are in it right now. The Church has always lived in the midst of great tribulation and persecution. It is nothing new. And it is certainly not coming. In fact, it is almost over. Our third-Day appointment to stand with the Son of Man in heaven has nearly arrived.

Blood-Washed Kings and Priests

The elder also informed John that this great multitude, gathered from every nation, tribe, people, and tongue, "all washed their robes and made them white in the blood of the Lamb."

> Therefore, they are before the throne of God and serve Him day and night in His temple.

This eternal priestly service is the subject of the "new song," the song that only the 144 thousands can learn (have the right to sing).

It was first sung by the four living beings and the twenty-four elders when the Lamb received the Scroll from His Father's right hand.

Even though the tune remains a mystery, the words to the song are not; they were recorded in advance by John so that the Bride might understand her "heavenly calling."

> You are worthy to take the Scroll and to open its seals; for You were slain, and have redeemed us to God by Your blood out of every tribe and tongue and people and nation, and have made us kings and priests to our God; and we shall reign over the earth.[5]

We now have two witnesses concerning the coming of the Son of Man—the witness from the Mount of Olives and the witness from God's throne in heaven. Both witnesses agree and complement each other.

Both witnesses account for the same scenario of events leading up to the Lord's coming in the rapture at the end of this age. And both accounts conclude with the Church fully present in heaven as the last half of Daniel's seventieth week begins.

The fourteenth chapter of the book of Revelation opens by saying,

> Then I looked, and behold, a Lamb standing on Mount Zion, and with Him one hundred and forty-four thousands, having His Father's name written on their foreheads.
>
> And I heard a voice from heaven, like the voice of many waters, and like the voice of loud thunder. And I heard the sound of harpists playing their harps.

---

[5]   Revelation 5:9–10

The next verse says,

> They sang as it were a new song before the
> throne, before the four living creatures, and the
> elders; and no one could learn that song except
> the hundred and forty-four thousands who were
> redeemed from the earth.[6]

---

[6]   Revelation 14:1–3

25

Living in Father's House

The dialogue between John and the elder was intentionally orchestrated by God. It was not just a casual conversation that took place during a lull in the vision. Instead, the elder was specifically sent to reveal some important things about the Bride, *including where she will live.*

As the conversation continues, I would like to quote the remainder of the elder's comments in verses 15–17 from the *Amplified Bible.*

> For this reason they are [now] before the [very] throne of God and serve Him day and night in His sanctuary [temple]; and He who is sitting upon the throne will protect and spread His tabernacle over and shelter them with His presence.
>
> They shall hunger no more, neither thirst anymore; neither shall the sun smite them, nor any scorching heat. For the Lamb who is in the midst of the throne will be their Shepherd, and He will guide them to the springs of the waters of life; and God will wipe away every tear from their eyes.

If this sounds similar to the twenty-third Psalm, it should; for the psalm was especially written with the Lord's elect in mind. We know this because the psalm concludes with the statement, *"and I will dwell in the house of the Lord forever."*

The "house of the Lord" refers to the heavenly Mount Zion and the city of the living God. It is the heavenly counterpart of the earthly Mount Zion in the land of Israel upon which the city of Jerusalem sits.

> But you have come to Mount Zion and to the city of the living God, the heavenly Jerusalem, to an innumerable company of angels, to the general assembly and church of the Firstborn who are registered in heaven, to God the Judge of all, to the spirits of just men made complete, to Jesus the Mediator of the new covenant, and to the blood of sprinkling that speaks better things than that of Abel.[1]

The twenty-first chapter of the book of Revelation provides a detailed description of this "Mountain City." For one thing, it is laid out as a square. Also, its length, width, and height are all equal. It is not a cube but more like a pyramid shaped in the form of a mountain. Therefore, it is called the heavenly Mount Zion.

The dimensions of its length, width, and height are comparable to the width of the United States as measured from the East Coast to the West Coast. So if you can imagine a mountain stretching across the entire width of our country but equally as high, you can begin to get a mental image of the vastness of this City.

It is a paradise, complete with all the landscapes with which we are so familiar but enhanced in a way that we can't possibly imagine. And if that doesn't blow your mind, it is quite possible that there are many levels *within* this Mountain just as we find in a multilevel shopping Mall.

---

[1]   Hebrews 12:22–24

Yet, because of the transparency of the City, each level feels open to the sky above. We would, therefore, dwell within this mountain city, not just on it. Obviously, the throne of God occupies the summit, or highest level. In short, this City is huge.

Jesus called it "His Father's House," saying, "In My Father's House are many mansions; if it were not so, I would have told you. I go to prepare a place for you. And if I go and prepare a place for you, I will come again and receive you to Myself, that where I am, there you may be also."

This special promise was made to His Bride—*to those who would believe on Him in between His departure and when He would come again.* As His "betrothed," we fall in between the phrases "I go to prepare a place for you" and "I will come again and receive you to Myself."

It is important to note that Jesus presently dwells in this heavenly City. He is present down here and "in our midst" *through the Person of the Holy Spirit.* It is, therefore, correct to say that Jesus is *there* and His Spirit is *here.*

This is important, for Jesus did not say, "I will come again, that where we are, *here* He might be also." Instead, He said, "That where I am, *there* you may be also."

Most people do not understand the second coming of Christ. They don't understand that His return to gather His Bride in the rapture *is the second coming.* Instead, they confuse His subsequent descent at the battle of Armageddon with "the second coming." They think that "His coming" is all about Him being present on the earth *rather than His Bride being present with Him in heaven.*

Later on, we will see how Jesus will reign with His Bride from above in the heavenly Mount Zion. We will also see how He will maintain His Presence here on the earth, especially in the midst of Israel, through the Person of the Holy Spirit.

Today, Jesus is in our midst because of the "early rains," the outpouring of His Spirit that began on the Feast of Pentecost nearly two thousand years ago. During His thousand-year reign, His Presence on the earth will be accomplished through a "latter-rain" outpouring.

For now, it is important to see that *the purpose of Him coming again is to take us to be with Him,* not so that He might come and dwell upon the earth. Once He comes in the rapture, *it can be said that the Lord has come.*

Together, we will temporarily leave His Father's House several years later to descend at the battle of Armageddon. The purpose of this brief excursion is nothing more than to finalize His wrath by consigning Satan to the Pit and the Antichrist to the Lake of Fire.

Once these things have been accomplished, we will return with Jesus to our "prepared place," *for it is our destiny to dwell in the house of the Lord forever.* Jesus did not prepare this place just to leave it vacant for the remainder of the thousand years.

Therefore, Jesus is coming back so that we might be there with Him, not that He might be here with us. This is the truth that the elder revealed to John. The Lamb *who is in the midst* of the throne will shepherd us. Psalm 99:1–2 says,

> The Lord reigns, let the peoples tremble! He dwells between the cherubim; let the earth be moved! The Lord is great in Zion, and He is high above all the peoples...

All of the Scriptures that address His coming emphasize the truth that *His Bride will live with Him,* not that He will come to live on the earth. Paul understood this, for after describing the rapture in 1 Thessalonians 4, the chapter ends with, "And thus, we shall always *be with the Lord.*"

He reiterated this point later in chapter 5, verse 10, when he said, "Who died for us, that whether we wake or sleep, we should *live together with Him.*" In Colossians 3:4, he wrote, "When Christ who is our life appears, then you also will appear *with Him in glory.*"

In John 12:26, Jesus said, "If anyone serves Me, let him follow Me; and where I am, *there My servant will be also.*"

As the 144 thousands, we will follow the Lamb wherever He goes, even when He descends to the battle of Armageddon. But as far as where He lives, He dwells between the Cherubim in Heaven;

or as the elder put it, the Lamb *who is in the midst* of the throne will Shepherd them. In short, *He is coming to take us home.*

Even though the Old Testament saints also dwell in the heavenly Mount Zion, the Scriptures make it clear that the City was prepared especially for the Lamb's Bride. This explains why John saw the City when he was told that he would see the Bride in the following passage from Revelation 21:9–10:

> Then one of the seven angels… came to me and talked with me, saying, "Come, and I will show you the bride, the Lamb's wife." And he carried me away in the Spirit to a great and high mountain, and showed me the great city, the holy Jerusalem, descending out of heaven from God.

To see the Bride is to see the City; and to see the City is to see the Bride. This is because it will be our permanent Home. After the millennium, this city will descend to join with earth in a new heavens and a new earth.

The truth that we will dwell in our Father's house forever means that various passages in the Psalms were meant to be taken literally, *not just spiritually.* Psalm 91 for example, begins, "He who dwells in the secret place of the Most High shall abide under the shadow of the Almighty."

Notice that the emphasis is that we will *abide* under His shadow, just as the four living beings and the twenty-four elders do. We will literally live in the shadow of His presence. This secret place is not only the place of highest service, but the place of highest authority as well.

Psalm 31:20 says, "You shall hide them in the secret place of Your presence." This place is reserved for the richest of blessings, for Psalm 16:11 reveals, "In Your presence is fullness of joy; at Your right hand are pleasures forevermore."

26

Dwelling in His Holy Hill

In Psalm 15:1, David asked an important question worth pondering: "Lord, who may abide in Your tabernacle? Who may dwell in Your holy hill?" The elder answered this question for us when he queried John as to the identity of the great multitude standing before God's throne.

> Then one of the elders answered, saying to me, "Who are these arrayed in white robes, and where did they come from?" And I said, "Sir, you know."
>
> So he said to me, "These are the ones who come out of the great tribulation, and washed their robes and made them white in the blood of the Lamb."
>
> Therefore they are before the throne of God, and serve Him day and night in His temple. And He who sits on the throne will dwell among them.

There are three main reasons why the great multitude depicted in the sixth seal will live in the house of the Lord forever. First, as the Lamb's wife, *our marriage to the Bridegroom* means that we will live with Him in His Father's House. Second, *as spiritual priests*, we will serve God day and night in His sanctuary. And third, *as servant-kings*, our rightful place is none other than at the Father's right hand.

The new song of the 144 thousands revealed that the One who was worthy to open the Scroll has made us to be "kings and priests to our God." The elder confirmed this heavenly calling by revealing that we will serve God day and night in His temple.

This priestly calling "after the order of Melchizedek" will require our continued presence before God's throne in the heavenly Mount Zion. The phrase "day and night in His temple" simply means that we are all called "full time" to this ministry.

This does not mean however that we must all stand there worshipping nonstop from that time forward. Instead, it means that at any time, day or night, some of us will always be found there functioning in this capacity. It means that a contingent from among this great multitude will always be present.

Since we will have other responsibilities to discharge as well, ours will be a full and rich life, composed of both rest and service.

The phrase "serving in His temple" also deserves some consideration. Later in the book of Revelation, John wrote, "But I saw no temple in it [the Heavenly Jerusalem], for the Lord God Almighty and the Lamb are its temple."[1]

This means that our spiritual service will not be confined to a mere building, for this is a spiritual temple. It means that we will serve "in the Presence of God and the Lamb." Not only that, *the truth that this City has a Temple* proves that we will serve *from above during the thousand years*, not down below on the earth. We know this because "the Temple" is also composed of "living stones." In 1 Peter 2:5, Peter wrote,

---

[1]   Revelation 21:22

> You also, as living stones, are being built up a
> spiritual house, a holy priesthood, to offer spiri-
> tual sacrifices…

In Ephesians 2:21, Paul revealed that Jesus Christ is the chief cornerstone of this Temple, "in whom the whole building, being fitted together grows into a holy temple in the Lord." We will not only serve "in the Temple," *for we will be an integral part of that City's Temple.*

Among the many promises made to those who overcome, Revelation 3:12 states, "He who overcomes, I will make him *a pillar* in the temple of My God, *and he shall go out no more.*"

Just as a pillar is a featured part of the Temple, our abiding presence will be a standard feature of the City. Together with God the Father, and Jesus the Lamb, this City's Temple will also include us. As pillars, *we will go out no more.*

This does not mean that we can never leave for an occasional appearance on the earth from time to time. Heaven is not the "Hotel California." In fact, we know that we will temporarily descend with Christ at the battle of Armageddon.

The point is this: *how can the City have a Temple if we are all absent dwelling full time on the earth?* Even though an earthly counterpart of the Temple will be built for those who live on the earth, we must remain in heaven for the Heavenly Tabernacle to be complete.

The promise in Revelation 3:12 not only states that we will "go out no more" but continues by saying, "And I will write on him the name of the City of My God."

The name of that great City would not be "written upon us" unless it is our permanent address. Just as your current address is stamped on your driver's license, the New Jerusalem will be inscribed upon us as being our current place of residence. And since we will dwell at this address forever, this will never change—not during the thousand years of Christ's reign *and* not for all eternity.

Over the Earth, Not "on" the Earth

Many have wondered whether the final stanza of the new song in Revelation 5:10 means that we will reign *on the earth* or *over the earth*. Some translations say "on" the earth, some say "upon," while others say "over" the earth. *The Interlinear Greek-English New Testament* has "on (? over)," indicating that the Greek in this instance is unclear.

When we let Scripture interpret Scripture, we find that the answer is "over the earth." We will live in our Father's House as the Bride of Christ. As priests before God, we will serve as part of the City's Temple. And as kings, we will rule from the Father's right hand.

It is a common misconception that Jesus must physically remain on the earth in order to effectively reign during His millennial rule. But this is not what the Scriptures teach. It is only what we have assumed by leaning on our natural understanding. If you think about it, the same situation exists today relative to the powers of darkness.

Right now, Satan is the god of this world system. He rules from the realm of the unseen. He rules with wicked spirits in "high places," which in Greek means "elevations" or "above the sky." If Satan can rule from somewhere up above, cannot Jesus and His coheirs rule from above also?

According to the book of Revelation, Michael and his angels will cast Satan and his angels out of their "high places" down to the earth as Daniel's seventieth week resumes. At that time, Satan will have great wrath, knowing that his time is short (the final three and a half years of Daniel's seventieth week). After that, Satan will be confined to the pit for the remainder of the thousand years.

This means that for the remainder of Christ's reign, there will be no interference from wicked spirits operating in between God's throne above and His footstool down below. They will all be bound.

I conclude then that we will reign over the earth from our heavenly position at the Father's right hand. Earthly assignments will be carried out on our behalf by the angels—"those ministering spirits sent forth to minister for those who have inherited salvation" according to Hebrews 1:14.

Another point that favors "ruling from above" concerns the prediction in Revelation 20:7–10. The passage reveals how Satan will be loosed for a "short season" at the end of the thousand years to deceive the nations one final time. How could the nations possibly be deceived if Jesus is ruling on the earth in His glorious visible form?

On the other hand, if He is ruling from the realm of the unseen, from the heavenly Mount Zion, then this last "test" makes sense. By then, the Lord's return and the battle of Armageddon will be ancient history, just like His first coming is to us today.

Since people will be born during the thousand years who never witnessed these events, the fact of Christ's first *and second coming* will become a question of faith. They will have to walk by faith and not by sight just as we do today. Therefore, Satan will be loosed for a brief time to test what they really believe. The people in that time will have to do what we did:

> That the genuineness of your faith, being much
> more precious than gold that perishes, though it
> is tested by fire, may be found to praise, honor,
> and glory at the revelation of Jesus Christ, whom
> having not seen you love. Though now you do
> not see Him, yet believing, you rejoice with joy
> inexpressible and full of glory.[2]

In summary, we can all agree that Christ will effectively rule the earth during the thousand years. Personally, it fills my heart with great comfort knowing that I will dwell in the house of the Lord forever under the watchful care of the Good Shepherd.

After all, I'd rather spend one Day in His courts as a doorkeeper than a thousand anywhere else, wouldn't you!

---

[2]   1 Peter 1:7–8

27

———✦✕✕✦———

A Day in Your Courts

Better is one Day in your courts than a thousand elsewhere. (Ps. 84:10)

Did you know that the eighty-fourth Psalm depicts the rapture? Did
you know that it was written to Jesus's Bride—the innumerable multitude that the elder told John about?

I remember the day when I saw it. I was out in my garage with
our eldest son, Vaughn, and we were just preaching back and forth
to each other. Somehow, the Lord led us to the eighty-fourth Psalm.

Vaughn had his "fancy Bible" with all the Greek and Hebrew
words in the back and was looking up various words as we examined
each verse. By the time we were finished, we both stood amazed. I
said, "I never saw this before. This is all about the rapture!"

The psalm begins,

How lovely are your tabernacles, O Lord of hosts!
My soul yearns, yes, even pines and is homesick
for the courts of the Lord; my heart and my flesh
cry out and sing for joy to the living God.

I like the way the *Amplified Bible* translates this opening verse. It points out that we can call the courts of His tabernacle *our home*. If that doesn't make you sing for joy, nothing will! The psalm continues,

> Even the sparrow has found a home, and the swallow a nest for herself, where she may have her young—a place near your altar, O Lord Almighty, my King and my God.
>
> Blessed are those who dwell in your house; they are ever praising you. (NIV)

The psalmist is saying that even the tiniest, most insignificant creatures have a home, for God provides for each and every one of them. The praise of the psalmist reaches a crescendo upon the thought that we have a home too—in our Father's house of many mansions.

The next part of the psalm links with the passage in Isaiah 40, wherein those who "yearn" or wait upon the Lord will "pass on to strength" and mount up with wings as eagles. Or as the psalmist put it, "Blessed are those whose strength is in you, who have set their hearts on pilgrimage." The *Amplified Bible* reads, "In whose heart are the highways to Zion." The psalm continues,

> Passing through the Valley of Weeping (Baca), they make it a place of springs; the early rain also fills [the pools] with blessings. They go from strength to strength [increasing in victorious power]; each of them appears before God in Zion.

As believers, our hearts should be set on pilgrimage. We know that this world is not our real home. *And even though it is needful to stay until our work here is finished,* our hearts should often yearn for the courts of the Lord. It is not wrong to occasionally feel "homesick" and to joyfully anticipate the time when we can finally go home to be with the Lord.

My mother went home to be with the Lord in her mideighties. During her final months, and after suffering a stroke, my wife and I brought her to our home so that she could live with us and be taken care of. Even though it was difficult, it was very rewarding. She cared for me when I was young, and now I had the privilege to care for her.

I remember the times when we would sit at her bed, and she would ask us to pray, saying, "Pray that the Lord will take me home tonight. I know that it's time for me to go, and I'm ready." She had lived a full life and missed my dad who had departed several years earlier. She just wanted to go home. So early one morning, the Lord answered her prayer. She didn't really die; she simply stepped over into a realm of life far richer than we can dare to imagine.

Until the rapture happens, there is still only one way to get home. Believers must pass through the "valley of the shadow of death" as David poetically wrote in the twenty-third Psalm. He assured us that there is nothing to fear in this valley, for the Good Shepherd remains by our side. His rod and staff comforts us while we make this fateful journey. Nevertheless, the valley is presently known as the "valley of weeping" for the loved ones left behind.

All that changes in Psalm 84, for the psalm depicts believers passing through this valley in the rapture. No longer a dry valley of sorrow, it becomes a "place of springs" with "pools of blessings." The quickening presence of the Holy Spirit, typified by the "early rains," will enable us to pass on with His impartation of strength. We will "go from strength to strength," that is, from the strength of mortality to the strength of immortality. This enabling strength will cause "each of us to appear before God in Zion."

Even though the valley was known for weeping when our departed loved ones previously passed through it, the departure of living believers will be different when the Lord returns. For one thing, no one will cry at your funeral, not because they didn't like you, *but because there won't be a funeral in the first place!*

Like Enoch and Elijah, we will skip the funeral altogether, fly through the valley rejoicing, only to appear before God in Zion. You will know you are finally home when the Father calls you by name and invites you to sit on His lap so that He can love on you to your heart's delight. He will look on you with favor, because this is how He looks on Jesus, His anointed One.

Verse 11 echoes the sentiments of the elder who conversed with John, for the psalmist prophesied, "For the Lord God is a sun and shield; the Lord bestows favor and honor; no good thing does He withhold from those whose walk is blameless."

Likewise, the elder told John, "They shall hunger no more, neither thirst anymore; neither shall the sun smite them, nor any scorching heat. For the Lamb who is in the midst of the throne will be their Shepherd, and He will guide them to the springs of the waters of life; and God will wipe away every tear from their eyes."

Notice that the Lamb is not in the midst of the earth *but in the midst of the throne*. This means that our true home is up there, not down here. He will shepherd us from the midst of God's throne and in the mountain paradise of His city. This is our "nesting place," a place near the altar of our God and King. It will be a place of lush green pastures, beautiful landscapes, and abundant rivers of living water. There, the scorching heat of the sun will never smite us again. Instead, we will be warmly bathed in the sunshine of His glory and love.

For those who are younger and feel that the Lord's return will cause them to miss out on the things of this life, fear not, for no good thing will the Lord withhold from you once you come home. In fact, He will bestow you with favor and honor throughout eternity. You won't feel that you missed out on a single thing.

A Day to a Thousand

I intentionally skipped the tenth verse of Psalm 84 so that we could look at it last. It says, "Better is one Day in your courts than a thousand elsewhere; I would rather be a doorkeeper in the house of My God than dwell in the tents of the wicked."

The prophetic element in such Psalms becomes even more apparent the better acquainted we become with other scriptures in the Bible. The intentional contrast of "one Day" to "a thousand" was mentioned in order to steer us to the following passage in Peter's second epistle:

> Nevertheless, do not let this one fact escape your notice, beloved, that with the Lord one Day is as a thousand years and a thousand years as one Day.[1]

Why would the Holy Spirit speak of spending one Day in His courts in a passage about "coming home" in the rapture—especially when we know that this will be our home throughout eternity? Why did God single out one Day out of all eternity?

We know that the Lord's thousand-year reign will begin once He comes to take His Bride to heaven. We also know that this begins the "last Day" of God's great Week. Once this last Day is finished, the prophetic divisions of the "times and seasons" will not be necessary, for God will create a new heavens and a new earth. Once this occurs, we will enter eternity future. But until that time comes, one last prophetic marker remains. In Acts 17:31, this last Day is also called "the appointed Day"—the Day in which God will judge (or rule) the earth "by the Man" whom He has ordained.

> Because He has appointed a Day on which He will judge the world in righteousness by the Man whom He ordained. He has given assurance of this to all by raising Him from the dead.

Our first book revealed how this "ordained Man" refers to Jesus as the head, and the Church as His body. Together, and as God's firstborn Son, we will rule over the earth in the Day that lasts a thousand years.

---

[1]   2 Peter 3:8 (Amplified Bible)

Therefore, according to Psalm 84, even a "doorkeeper" dwelling in the "House of God" *will have more authority in that Day than any head of state down below!*

28

The Purpose behind His Parousia

Our failure to understand that Jesus was teaching about the rapture in His Olivet Discourse, not the battle of Armageddon, made Christ's second coming difficult to understand. End-time prophecy teachers (myself included) saw the terms *abomination of desolation* and *great tribulation* and were convinced that we were reading about the last half of a "future seven-year tribulation."

Because of this, we lost much of what Jesus taught about His coming in the rapture. Over time, it devolved into a secret and sign-less event. Before long, we had two future "comings," one secret and one visible. If that wasn't confusing enough, "the second coming" became identified with the battle of Armageddon rather than Christ's visible descent in the rapture *several years earlier*.

Having studied what the Bible says about the Lord's return for much of my adult life, I am convinced that the New Testament writers linked the rapture with Christ's second coming. They understood that there was only one "second coming," and that He was coming again so that His Bride might be present with Him in heaven. Today, we have made the second coming to be all about the battle of Armageddon. In short, we have confused "His coming" with "His reigning." We think that it is all about Jesus being present here on the earth, when it is actually about His Bride being present with Him in Glory.

Jesus's reign over the nations could have begun the moment He ascended into heaven nearly two thousand years ago. The only reason it didn't is He is waiting for His coruling Bride to fully join Him at His Father's right hand—literally. Only then can His reign over the nations begin.

The truth that there is only one second coming can be understood by noting the various Greek words used to describe His coming. These words, together with their meanings, are as follows:

1. *parousia*—present with
2. *erchomai*—the act of coming or going
3. *apokalupsis* —revealing
4. *epiphaneia*—appearing
5. *phaneroo*—manifestation
6. *optomai*—to be seen

It should be noted that all of these Greek words are used in passages that clearly depict the rapture. For example, Paul wrote, "For this we say to you by the word of the Lord, that we who are alive and remain until the coming (*parousia*) of the Lord will by no means precede those who are asleep."[1]

Parousia is a compound word that means "being with" or "presence." Jesus will come so that His Bride can *remain with Him*, not so that He can remain on the earth.

Jesus used the same word in His Olivet Discourse when He compared His visible return with the flashing of lightning, saying, "So also will the coming (*parousia*) of the Son of Man be."

A few verses later, He used the words *erchomai* (the act of coming or going) and *optomai* (to see) when He said, "then all the tribes of the earth will mourn, and they will see (*optomai*) the Son of Man coming (*erchomai*) on the clouds of heaven." Therefore, the word

---

[1]   1 Thessalonians 4:15

parousia is used to describe the rapture *and His visible return*. This is because it is all one event.

The word *apokalupsis* means "unveiling" and "revealing." In I Corinthians 1:7, Paul wrote to believers saying, "So that you come short in no gift, eagerly waiting for the revelation (*apokalupsis*) of our Lord Jesus Christ, who will also confirm you to the end, that you may be blameless in the Day of our Lord Jesus Christ."

Peter added, "And rest your hope fully upon the grace that is to be brought to you at the revelation (*apokalupsis*) of Jesus Christ."[2] Therefore, when Jesus comes in His *parousia*, He will also be revealed.

The word *epiphaneia* means "appearing" and "to shine forth." In 1 Timothy 6:14, Paul charged Timothy to "keep this commandment without spot, blameless until our Lord Jesus Christ's appearing (*epiphaneia*). Paul was not charging believers like Timothy to "keep this commandment" until Armageddon, but until the rapture.

Likewise, in Titus 2:13, he exhorted believers to be "looking for the blessed hope and glorious appearing (*epiphaneia*) of our great God and Savior Jesus Christ."

The word *phaneroo* simply means "to render apparent, to be manifested." In Colossians 3:4, we find, "When Christ who is our life appears (*phaneroo*), then you also will appear with Him in glory."

In 1 John 3:2, the disciple whom Jesus loved added, "Beloved, now we are children of God; and it has not yet been revealed what we shall be, but we know that when He is revealed (*phaneroo*), we shall be like Him, for we shall see Him as He is."

Finally, the word *optomai* is used in Hebrews 9:28, "To those who eagerly wait for Him He will appear (*optomai*) a second time, apart from sin, for salvation."

When Jesus physically returns, He will appear, shine forth, be seen, be revealed, and be manifested. Above all, He will catch us up *to be with Him*. Clearly, all of these words are used in passages that describe the Lord's coming in the rapture. *And they are all written to His Bride.*

---

[2]   1 Peter 1:13

This is because the rapture *is the second coming.* Once His Bride has been gathered, it can be said that the Lord *has come.* It can also be said that the Day of the Lord has come. After that, any future dealings with the world, including the battle of Armageddon, involve the act of "reigning," not "coming."

Therefore, the purpose behind His *parousia* is so that His Bride *might be with Him in heaven.* The reason this is so vital is that He gave us His word that we would rule with Him. Therefore, His reign cannot begin *until those who will reign with Him are fully present and accounted for.*

The apostle Paul understood the difference between *coming* and *reigning* when he wrote,

> For as in Adam all die, even so in Christ all shall be made alive. But each one in his own order [or company]: Christ the firstfruits, then, those who are Christ's at His coming.

> Then comes the end, when He [Jesus] delivers the Kingdom to God the Father, when He puts an end to all rule and all authority and power; for He must reign till He has put all enemies under His feet. The last enemy that will be destroyed is death.[3]

Paul defined *reigning* as the act of putting every enemy underfoot. This thousand-year reign will continue until death, the last enemy to be put underfoot, has been destroyed.

Many in the Church have confused the act of putting every enemy underfoot with His coming. They are not the same thing. His coming is one thing; treading is another. Once His Bride has been fully gathered and united with Him, only then can the treading begin.

---

[3]   1 Corinthians 15:24–26

Therefore, the battle of Armageddon does not mark the time of the Lord's return, but the time when the Antichrist will be put underfoot. This "treading" will span three and a half years—the last half of Daniel's seventieth week. It will continue until even death has been destroyed.

29

How His Treading Begins

The distinction between the "Lord's coming" and "His treading" can be seen in a prophecy from Isaiah. In chapter 24, verse 17 begins, "Fear and the pit and the snare are upon you, O inhabitant of the earth…" Jesus cautioned us not to let that Day come upon us unexpectedly, saying, "For it will come as a snare on all those who dwell on the face of the whole earth."[1] He promised that watchful believers will "escape all these things" to stand in His presence by eagerly looking for His return.

So at this point in Isaiah's prophecy, the Lord has already come, and the rapture has already occurred. Those who belonged to Christ at His coming have escaped to stand before the Son of Man, and the snare has come upon the inhabitants of the earth.

As the prophecy continues, Isaiah describes what will happen once the Day of the Lord begins, and this snare comes upon the earth.

> It shall come to pass in that Day that the Lord
> will punish on high the host of exalted ones; and

---

[1]   Luke 21:34–35

> on the earth, the kings of the earth. They will be gathered together, as prisoners are gathered in the pit, and will be shut up in the prison; after many days they will be punished.

Once the Lord comes in that Day, His treading will begin. Isaiah reveals that the Lord will do two things. First, He will proceed to "punish on high the host of exalted ones." The *host of exalted ones* refers to the spiritual powers who currently preside over the earth. The apostle Paul described them as being "the rulers of the darkness of this world" and "spiritual hosts of wickedness in the heavenly realms above this earth."[2]

The passage in Revelation 12:7–9 reveals how Michael and his angels will assist in accomplishing this punishment. As the last half of Daniel's seventieth week begins, an angelic war will be fought in the heavens above our planet. Michael and his angels will cast the devil and his angels down to the earth. At this point, the devil will know that his time is short.

Second, Jesus will also punish "the kings of the earth." This refers to the nations who will come against Israel. This punishment is depicted by the seven trumpets and bowls of the book of Revelation.

At the end of the three and a half years, Jesus will then proceed to fulfill the last part of Isaiah's prophecy. These kings and exalted ones will be "gathered together, as prisoners are gathered in the pit, and will be shut up in the prison." *This is what Jesus's descent with the armies of heaven at Armageddon is all about.* The devil and his angels will be cast into "the pit"; and the kings of the earth, including the Antichrist, will be destroyed and cast into the Lake of Fire. This final act of treading is depicted in Revelation 19:11–21.

There is nothing in Scripture to indicate that either Jesus or His Bride will stay to live on the earth for the remainder of the thousand years. In fact, the Bible reveals that we will reign from up above in our Father's House. Together, we will continue to reign from up above until every enemy has been put under His feet, including death itself.

---

[2]   Ephesians 6:12

So just to be clear, the second coming of Christ (and the rapture) will occur several years before our subsequent descent at the battle of Armageddon. Therefore, the purpose behind Jesus's coming is so that His Bride can be "with Him" in His Father's House.

In contrast, the purpose behind our descent several years later at the battle of Armageddon is to "gather and imprison" the host of exalted ones and the kings of the earth. By then both enemies will have been put underfoot. This is the difference between "coming" and "reigning."

So the scenario of events will go like this: the Lord will come a second time to fulfill the prophecy concerning the last half of Daniel's seventieth week. When Jesus comes, He will stand on the Mount of Olives and split it in two. This will foil the invasion of the Antichrist as he leads his forces against the land of Israel.

Jesus will then receive His Church, Body, and Bride to heaven that we might stand in His Presence. Jesus will reenact His ascension, only this time with His Body (the Church) now complete. Thus, we will escape the snare of that Day.

Israel, on the other hand, will not escape. Instead, they will flee through the "mountain valley" that will be created when Jesus splits Mount Zion. They will be kept and protected for the remaining three and a half years. (This is fully explained in our second book, *Daniel's Seventieth Week*.)

With His Bride now with Him in heaven, the Lord will then proceed to fight against the nations. He will punish them by striking them with the rod of His wrath. After three and a half years He will descend with the armies of heaven to cast the Antichrist into the Lake of Fire and Satan into the pit.

Then the Lord will keep His promise to the children of Israel. He will establish the throne of David upon the earth. They will be the head and not the tail. He will appoint them to stand at the head of the nations and rule from the city of Jerusalem. It will become a city of renown, earth's capital city, and the center of worship and instruction throughout all the earth.

With earth's delegated government in place, we return to our Father's House and continue to reign from above. Our authority will be administered in a way similar to the Roman Centurion who came to Jesus on behalf of his servant. The Centurion recognized that Jesus had the authority to heal his servant, even though the servant was not physically present.

> But only speak the word and my servant will be healed; for I also am a man under authority, having soldiers under me. And I say to this one, "Go," and he goes; and to another, "Come," and he comes; and to my servant, "Do this," and he does it.[3]

As heaven's centurions, we will have "soldiers" and "servants" to help us administer heaven's authority over the earth. In Hebrews 1:14, the writer revealed the identity of these "holy helpers," by saying,

> But to which of the angels has He ever said, "Sit at My right hand, till I make your enemies your footstool?" Are they not all ministering spirits sent forth to minister for those who will inherit salvation?

As ministering spirits, the angels will carry out our "Centurion commands" in the age to come. This is what Paul meant in 1 Corinthians 6:2–3 when he told believers, "Do you not know that the saints will judge (rule) the world... do you not know that we shall judge angels?"

He did not mean that we will be deciding the fate of the fallen angels, for God has already judged them. Instead, he was referring to the angels that remained faithful to God. They will lovingly work with us to administer God's authority over the cities on the earth that God has placed under our care.

---

[3]   Matthew 8:8–9

According to Luke 19:17, in that Day Jesus will say to His joint heirs (faithful believers), "Well done good and faithful servant…have authority over ten cities." Just because we are in heaven does not mean that we cannot effectively rule the earth. And just because we might have authority over ten cities doesn't mean that we have to live there.

In summary, we can effectively rule from above. Nor will our rule put God's angels "out of business." Together, we will have plenty to do during that "Day in His courts." And we can still visit the earth as needed even though we live in our Father's House. It is going to be awesome!

Therefore, Isaiah's prophecy concludes by saying, "For the Lord of hosts will reign on Mount Zion and in Jerusalem *and before His elders gloriously.*"

30

The Seating of the Court

Unless we understand the Scriptures, we will confuse the second *parousia* of Christ with His treading at the battle of Armageddon. We need to see the big picture in that the Lord will (1) come, then (2) punish, and ultimately (3) imprison and destroy.

It is also important to understand how the Lord's *parousia*, His coming to take His Bride to be present with Him in glory, *is vitally necessary in order to punish and destroy the kings who are on the earth.*

Long ago, the prophet Daniel was given a vision to explain just why this is so. I call it "the seating of the court," and it appears in the seventh chapter of Daniel.

The vision depicts four great beasts coming up out of the sea (the nations) to oppose and oppress the nation of Israel. The first is the kingdom of Babylon (the lion), the second is the kingdom of Persia (the bear), the third is the kingdom of Greece (the leopard), and the fourth is the kingdom of Rome (an exceedingly strong beast).

The interpretation of Nebuchadnezzar's dream in Daniel 2 depicts these same Gentile kingdoms. The dream not only revealed that this fourth kingdom would become bitterly divided between East and West (the two legs), *but that it would continue until it is utterly destroyed once Christ returns.* Therefore, both divisions of this kingdom *extend into our present time.*

The subsequent vision in chapter 7 was specifically given to show how this "two-legged kingdom" will be destroyed by the coming of the Son of Man. *Most critically, it reveals why the Bride must be seated with her Husband in order for this judgment to be accomplished.*

Since this vision concerns the generation that will witness the Lord's return, the main focus of the vision zeroes in on our time. It shows the rise of the Antichrist (depicted as the little horn) in verse 8 and his destruction in verse 11.

The coming of the Lord in the rapture appears in verses 9 and 10, in between the rise and fall of the little horn. The rapture is depicted by a "fiery stream" that issues forth from God that suddenly fetches "a thousand thousands, and ten thousand times ten thousand" to "stand before Him."

This part of the vision corresponds to what John saw in Revelation 7 concerning *the 144 thousands* and the *great multitude* standing before God's throne. It also links with John's vision of the seven-sealed Scroll—the decree that authorizes Christ and His coheirs to take possession of the kingdoms of the earth. We see this as the vision continues in Daniel 7:13–14:

> I was watching in the night visions, and behold, One coming like the Son of Man, coming with the clouds of Heaven! He came to the Ancient of Days [the Father] and they brought Him near before Him.
>
> Then to Him was given dominion and glory and a kingdom that all peoples, nations, and languages should serve Him.

It is important to note that Jesus was given "all authority and power, both in heaven and earth" when He was raised from the dead and seated at the Father's right hand nearly two thousand years ago.

Yet He did not take immediate possession of the earth at that time, even though He could have. Why not?

It is because God had a greater plan in mind. The Father decided to give King Jesus, the Son of Man, a heavenly Esther, a newfound Bride to sit with Him on His throne. The preparation and seating of this Bride is the reason for the two-Day delay. In short, she needs to be seated before the "clay pot" Gentile kingdoms can be broken.

Someone might contend, "But aren't we already seated with Christ?" The answer is yes and no. In a spiritual sense, it is true that believers have been "raised up together and made to sit together in the heavenly places in Christ." Paul taught these things in Ephesians 2:4–6.

Even though this is a *spiritual reality* that yields great benefits in this life, it will become our full and complete experience at the *parousia*, or coming of Jesus Christ.

Presently, our lives are *hidden in Him*, just as the entire human race was once hidden in Adam. But when the second and last Adam comes (Christ), we will be "manifested" such that our spiritual realities "in Him" become our ultimate experience in the House of the Lord.

This is what John meant when He said, "Beloved, now we are children of God; and it has not yet been revealed what we shall be, but we know that when He is revealed, we shall be like Him, for we shall see Him as He is."

This point is an emphatic part of the revelation to be gained from Daniel's vision. The vision reveals how the Son of Man will come so that His joint heirs can be *officially and literally* seated with Him at His Father's throne as part of heaven's judicial court.

In the vision, these thrones were "put in place" back in verse 9, before our seizure in the rapture by the fiery stream of verse 10. With Christ's body standing complete and before the throne, verse 10 concludes by saying, "The court was seated and the books were opened."

As joint heirs with Christ, we will be officially seated as part of the government of heaven; we will be seated with Christ at the Father's right hand. We will have an assigned place in the midst of the four living beings and before the twenty-four elders. We will be called "*the general assembly* and Church of the Firstborn," according to the passage in Hebrews 12:23.

As kings and priests, we will be entitled to sing the "new song" and reign over the earth from our heavenly position of authority. We will do this for one Day—*and then for all eternity.*

Today, the Gospel is not only an offer of salvation *but an invitation to sit with God in heaven's throne.* In and of itself, the offer of redemption is *way more* than what we deserved, for we only deserved death and destruction; but to sit with God in His throne *as sons of the living God?* You would have to be out of your mind to reject such an offer.

Long ago, Lucifer was with God in heaven. He beheld God's glory in person. Yet he shunned God and tried to take God's throne by force. He deceived mankind in an attempt to aid him in this rebellion. In doing so, the devil enslaved us and tried to make us serve him.

But through His mercy and grace, God *freely offers His throne* to those who have never seen Him *yet believe in His goodness.* This explains why faith pleases God and why it is so important. Faith is the ultimate act of love and adoration from those who have never seen Him but believe only on the basis of His Word.

The Favorable Judgment

Returning to Daniel's vision, notice that once the court is seated in verse 10, the vision continues by saying, "I watched then because of the sound of the pompous words which the horn was speaking; I watched till the beast was slain, its body destroyed, and given to the burning flame." *This could not have happened unless the court had been seated.* Otherwise, Jesus would have broken the promise to His Bride that she will rule with Him.

We saw how Isaiah prophesied that the kings of the earth would be *punished and destroyed.* Now we know *how* and *when* this will happen. It will happen *when* Jesus comes to receive His Bride so that she can be seated as the "Heavenly Court."

As for the *how*, verses 22–27 reveal that this heavenly court will issue "a judgment" to "consume and destroy" the fourth beast, together with its bigmouthed little horn.

> I was watching; and the same horn was making war against the saints [Israel], and prevailing against them, until the Ancient of Days came, and a judgment was made in favor of the saints of the Most High, and the time came for the saints to possess the kingdom.

The truth that the fourth beast arose at the time of the Roman Empire *and has continued until its present form today* is an important point. Daniel was told that it would devour the whole earth, speak pompous words against the Most High, persecute the saints of the Most High, and intend to change times and law.

This was true of the Roman Empire back then, and it is still true today. True Christians have suffered under the eastern branch and the western branch for centuries. In the end, the little horn will seek to control both branches with a ten-horned confederation. Verse 25 continues,

> Then the saints shall be given into his hand for a time, times, and half a time.

The phrase "time, times, and half a time" means for a period spanning three and a half years. This sets the context of this part of the vision as being the last half of Daniel's seventieth week.

It should not surprise us to find "saints" living on the earth during the final few years of the Antichrist, for Israel's third-Day revival *will begin immediately after the rapture*. Their faith in Christ will "sanctify" them just as our faith does today.

Also, don't let the phrase "they will be given into his hand" fool you either. Revelation 13:4 says, "So they worshiped the dragon *who gave authority* to the beast." *God is not the One giving the saints into the hand of the Antichrist, the devil is.* In 2 Thessalonians 2:9, Paul wrote that "the coming of the lawless one is according to the working of Satan, with all power, signs, and lying wonders."

The devil will try to give Israel into the hands of the Antichrist during the last half of Daniel's seventieth week, but the next verse in Daniel reveals *why he will not succeed.*

> But the court will be seated and they shall take away his dominion, to consume and destroy it forever. Then the kingdom and dominion, and the greatness of the kingdoms under the whole heaven shall be given to the people, the saints of the Most High.

Note the words *consume* and *destroy*, for Paul used these same two words when he wrote, "And then the lawless one will be revealed, whom the Lord will *consume* with the breath of His mouth and *destroy* with the brightness (*epiphaneia*) of His coming (*parousia*).[1]

Together with the Lion of the tribe of Judah, the court will render a verdict for God's angels to consume and destroy: *to consume* gradually with wrath for three and a half years and *to destroy* suddenly at the end when Christ and His armies *shine forth* from heaven.

In summary, Daniel's vision reveals that this "little horn," together with the fourth beast, will not be destroyed until the Lord's *parousia* (second coming), when His Bride is taken to be present with Him in glory to be seated as the heavenly court.

When Jesus ascended to heaven, His Father said, "Sit at My right hand until I make your enemies your footstool. I will send the rod of your strength out of Zion. Rule in the midst of your enemies... you shall execute kings in the Day of My wrath. You shall judge among the nations."[2]

The four winds represent part of this wrath. They were set to be released to harm the earth way back in John's time. But the four angels were told to wait and hold them back. It wasn't time yet. Jesus,

---

[1]   2 Thessalonians 2:8

[2]   Psalm 110:1–5

the "rod of His strength," had not yet been sent out; and His coheirs had not yet been gathered and seated.

But once that "fiery stream" is sent forth, His heirs will be fully assembled. It is then that the court will officially be seated. *"And they shall take away the beast's dominion."*

This is the "hope of His calling"—and it is your "heavenly calling" as well. Will you rise up and answer the call? Will you take your assigned seat at the throne of his grace? Will you make your calling and election sure? Or will you forfeit that call, simply because you have to see Him first before you will believe?

31

As Promised

God always keeps His word. He made a covenant with Abraham and his descendants that Israel would be the head and not the tail—that they would stand at the head of the other nations. Therefore, when the dominion of the fourth beast is destroyed, "Then the greatness of the kingdoms *under* the whole heaven shall be given to *the people*, the saints of the Most High"—as promised.

Likewise, in Revelation 3:21, Jesus sent a message to His Church, saying, "To him who overcomes I will grant to sit with Me on My throne, as I overcame and sat down with My Father on His throne." So in Daniel 7, we saw a fiery stream fetch multiplied thousands to appear before His throne so that the court could be seated—as promised.

When He was on the earth, Jesus promised that He would never leave us or forsake us, that He would be with us always, even to the end of the age. Yet the disciples watched *as He left* and was taken up to heaven. Again, He promised that He would be in our midst whenever two or three are gathered together in His name. How are these things possible when we know that He is presently seated at God's right hand?

The answer is simple. He sent another Comforter to abide with us forever. *He is present with us in the third Person of the Trinity, the Holy Spirit.* Since the very Spirit of God lives within us, we lost nothing when Jesus ascended. In fact, we gained everything. And even though Jesus is seated in heaven, He is still with us—as promised.

Similarly, Joel prophesied about Israel's glorious future, saying, "And My people shall never be put to shame. Then you shall know that *I am in the midst of Israel.*"[1]

Another Old Testament prophet saw a detailed vision of what the city of Jerusalem will be like when it is rebuilt during Christ's millennial reign. After describing what the city will look like, Ezekiel wrote, "And the name of the city from that Day shall be: *The Lord is there.*"[2]

Someone might ask, "But how can the Lord remain in heaven to rule *over the earth* when various passages make it sound like *He will be here instead?*"

The answer is the same as it is today with us. The Lord Himself dwells in heaven. He is seated at God's right hand. Yet He is also present here in our midst *because He poured out His Spirit on the Feast of Pentecost nearly two thousand years ago.* He has been here ever since in the Person of the Holy Spirit.

Long ago, Hosea prophesied,

> Let us know, let us pursue the knowledge of the Lord. His going forth is established as the morning; He will come to us like the rain, like the latter and former rain to the earth.

I realize that it is popular to think that we are presently living in the time of the latter rain. But are we? Hosea prophesied that the Messiah would come twice, just as there are two seasons of rain. When Jesus came the first time, it was followed by a season of rain

---

[1]   Joel 2:26–27

[2]   Ezekiel 48:35

called the early or former rains. God poured out His Spirit, and His Spirit has remained with us ever since.

We are born of His Spirit, are indwelt by His Spirit, are anointed with His Spirit, and should endeavor to live being filled with His Spirit. I thank God for His Spirit; for He leads us, He guides us, and He teaches us. He is here to strengthen us 24/7. Where would we be without the promise of this Divine Companion?

Yet both Joel and Hosea promised that there would be *a second outpouring*—a season that the Bible calls "the time of the latter rain." If Jesus is coming twice, why should the Holy Spirit be any different?

Just as Christ's first coming was followed by an outpouring called the former rains, His second coming will be followed by another outpouring—a latter-rain outpouring.

From our perspective, God has faithfully given us the former rain. It happened on the fifth of the seven Feasts of Israel, on the Day of Pentecost. Joel prophesied that God will cause the rain to come down again, a latter-rain outpouring in *the first month*.

The first month of Israel's civil calendar begins with the Feast of Trumpets. Later in the same month, they celebrate the seventh and last feast—the Feast of Tabernacles.

In 1 Corinthians 15:52, Paul linked the rapture with the "last trumpet blast" of the Feast of Trumpets. Since every eye will see the Lord when He returns, "even those that pierced Him,"[3] our departure will not only result in Israel's salvation but in a second outpouring as well. It will happen during the Feast of Tabernacles.

Zechariah prophesied that they will "look on the One they pierced" and mourn for Him "as one mourns for his only son" and "as one grieves for a firstborn." This time of national grieving will correspond to the Day of Atonement, a solemn day of repentance celebrated each year shortly after the Feast of Trumpets.

In all, there are seven feasts or "divine appointments" that God placed on their calendar. The first four were fulfilled at Christ's first coming. The last three will be fulfilled in one month's time when Jesus comes again.

---

[3]   Revelation 1:7

By then, the natural descendants of Abraham, Isaac, and Jacob will get it right. At His first coming, Jesus was presented as the only begotten of the Father. But when He comes again, He will be known as the Firstborn of many brethren. Thus, they will mourn "as one mourns for his only son" and grieve "as one grieves for a firstborn."

When that happens, Zechariah prophesied, "And I will pour on the house of David and on the inhabitants of Jerusalem the Spirit of grace and supplication."[4]

After the invasion of Israel and the battle of Armageddon (depicted in Ezekiel 38 and 39), Ezekiel also prophesied, "And I will not hide My face from them anymore; for I shall have poured out My Spirit on the house of Israel," says the Lord God.[5]

This latter-rain outpouring is further described in the tenth chapter of Zechariah. The chapter begins,

> Ask the Lord for rain in the time of the latter rain. The Lord will make flashing clouds; He will give them showers of rain and grass in the field for everyone.

Verse 2 reveals that they (Israel) have lacked rain and are in trouble *because there is no shepherd.* This all changes now that Jesus has appeared, and they finally embrace Him as their Good Shepherd.

With His anger kindled in verse 3, the Lord proceeds to "punish the goatherds." At this point in the chapter, He answers their latter-rain request with "a visitation of the Lord of Hosts," a second outpouring destined to be poured out upon the house of Judah. Verses 3–5 continue,

> And He will make the house of Judah as His royal horse in the battle... they shall be like mighty men who tread down their enemies in the mire of the streets in the battle. They shall fight because

---

4   Zechariah 12:10

5   Ezekiel 39:29

the Lord (His Spirit) is with them, and the riders
on horses will be put to shame.

Just as our former-rain outpouring enables us to tread on "spiritual serpents" and wrestle against principalities and powers, Israel's latter-rain outpouring will equip them to battle the forces of the Antichrist. They will be anointed for battle, just as the mighty men of the Old Testament era were endued with supernatural feats of strength. Verse 6 continues,

> I will strengthen the house of Judah and I will
> save the house of Joseph. I will bring them back
> and have mercy on them. They shall be as though
> I had not cast them aside; for I am the Lord their
> God, and I will hear them.

> Those of Ephraim shall be like a mighty man,
> and their hearts shall rejoice as if with wine. Yes,
> their children shall see it and be glad. Their heart
> shall rejoice in the Lord.

It will be a repeat of the Day of Pentecost, when those who were filled were drunk with "Holy Ghost wine." Only this time, it will happen at the Feast of Tabernacles. Even though the remainder of the chapter is well worth reading, I think you get the point. Because of the Lord's *parousia*, His Bride will be *present and seated with Him in heaven*. We will rule together *over the earth* from up above.

At the same time, the Lord will be present in the midst of His people *through His Spirit*. There will be a second outpouring as a result of His second coming—a latter-rain visitation to anoint the nation of Israel to tread and rule *on the earth*.

Many from among the Gentiles will also repent and believe as well. We know this because Zechariah 14:16 says, "And it shall come to pass that everyone who is left of all the nations which came against Jerusalem shall go up from year to year to worship the King."

Finally, Isaiah prophesied that in the last Days, "the mountain [kingdom] of the Lord's house shall be established on the top of the mountains [other nations] and shall be exalted above the hills; and all nations shall flow to it."[6]

> Many people shall come and say, "Come, and let us go up to the mountain of the Lord, to the house of the God of Jacob; He will teach us His ways and we shall walk in His paths.

In the end, the earth will flourish and enjoy her long-awaited Sabbath of millennial rest. Israel will stand at the head of the nations, and we will dwell in the house of the Lord forever—as promised!

---

[6]   Isaiah 2:2

The Emmaus Road Series

Emmaus Road is a collection of books heralding the soon return of Jesus Christ. The series is designed to restore what the Bible actually teaches about the rapture and the Lord's return. Many of these truths were either lost or diminished in later centuries. They are being restored at this time to ready the world for Christ's return.

Book 1: *See the Day Approaching*
Book 2: *Daniel's Seventieth Week*
Book 3: *The Coming of the Son of Man*

This series is dedicated to the Lord's Body of many members, to the living Stones of His glorious Temple, to the Church of the Firstborn, and to His adoring Bride as she awaits the coming of the Bridegroom.

If you want to know more about Chronos Ministries and our available resources, you may visit our website at http://www.chronos-ministries.org. You may also contact us at info@chronosministries.org.

About the Author

Jeffrey R. Horton together with his wife, Bonnie, are founders of Chronos Ministries based in Bradenton, Florida. Chronos Ministries is a Christ-centered teaching ministry preparing the Church for His soon return.

Jeffrey was called into the ministry in 1970. In the summer of 1983, he had an encounter with the Lord, in which Jesus said, "I want you to teach people about my return. As you teach, I want you to give them comfort, hope, and victory. If you will take the time to study, I will teach what you need to know." That encounter was the defining moment in his life. It became the mission of Chronos Ministries.

That call led to years of intensive Bible study and research and many Spirit-led question-and-answer sessions. It was Jeffrey's own Emmaus Road journey. Today, he shares what he learned about biblical end-time prophecies, the rapture, end-time events, the soon return of Jesus Christ, and our role as the Bride of Christ.

At Chronos Ministries, we believe the Holy Spirit is sponsoring a timely awakening on what the Bible really teaches about the Lord's return. It is a reforming work of His Spirit, returning us to the simplicity of God's Word. It is designed to unify and prepare the Body of Christ for a mighty end-time harvest and to enflame our hearts with a passionate desire for the coming Bridegroom.

CPSIA information can be obtained
at www.ICGtesting.com
Printed in the USA
FSOW01n0648300117
30086FS